No Magic Pill
Christian O'Reilly

T0228715

methuen | drama

LONDON • NEW YORK • OXFORD • NEW DELHI • SYDNEY

METHUEN DRAMA
Bloomsbury Publishing Plc
50 Bedford Square, London, WC1B 3DP, UK
1385 Broadway, New York, NY 10018, USA
29 Earlsfort Terrace, Dublin 2, Ireland

BLOOMSBURY, METHUEN DRAMA and the Methuen
Drama logo are trademarks of Bloomsbury Publishing Plc

First published in Great Britain 2022

A catalogue record for this book is available from the British Library.

A catalog record from this book is available from the Library of Congress.

ISBN: PB: 978-1-3503-7016-6
ePDF: 978-1-3503-7108-0
eBook: 978-1-3503-7107-3

Series: Modern Plays

Typeset by Mark Heslington Ltd, Scarborough, North Yorkshire

To find out more about our authors and books visit
www.bloomsbury.com and sign up for our newsletters.

No Magic Pill by Christian O'Reilly opened on 28 September 2022 at the Black Box, Galway with the following cast and creative team:

Ursula	Sorcha Curley
Brendan/Minister/Doctor/Physio Two/Vinny/Max	Mark Fitzgerald
Dermot	Peter Kearns
Mick/Albert/Sean	Ferdia MacAonghusa
Josie/Mother/Physio One/Sister	Julie Sharkey
Martin	Paddy Slattery

Director	Raymond Keane
Dramaturg & Disability Consultant	Peter Kearns
Set Designer	Ger Clancy
Lighting Designer	Sarah Jane Shiels
Costume Designer	Deirdre Dwyer
Composer and Sound Designer	Trevor Knight
Movement Director	Rachel Parry
Voice Coach	Andrea Ainsworth
Marketing Manager & Production Consultant	Hillary Dziminski
Production Manager	Marie Tierney
Stage Management	Donna Leonard and Róisín Ní Ghabhann
Publicity	Stephanie Dickenson
Marketing Consultant	Sinead McPhillips
Producers	Mitzi D'Alton and Christian O'Reilly

Presented in association with Town Hall Theatre, Galway and Civic Theatre, Dublin as part of Dublin Theatre Festival 2022.

Programme Notes

Judy Heumann, International Disability Rights Activist

My name is Judith (Judy) Heumann and I am a lifelong advocate for the rights of disabled people. Martin Naughton was a dear friend and leader and I am delighted that *No Magic Pill*, a stage play inspired by his life, is coming to fruition. Like Martin, I experienced discrimination at a young age and felt it was incumbent on me to collaborate with other disabled people in the US. As I began to meet other disabled people in countries around the world, we recognised that we were facing similar types of discrimination and had to begin to work together.

No Magic Pill will help to educate the community at large about the barriers disabled people face and the victories we must work so hard for. The absence of disability in the media is a major problem. When stories are not told, people are not learning. Having produced a paper for my Senior Fellowship with the Ford Foundation, 'A Road Map to Inclusion: Changing the Face of Disability in Media', I hear over and over again from disabled people how they feel invisible.

No Magic Pill will celebrate the life of a significant disability rights leader, one who deserves to be remembered in Ireland and internationally. By telling a story about disability, it will help to make disabled people feel visible.

I am excited to know that the production will feature a cast that includes disabled actors playing the disabled characters in the play. This should be the norm in Irish theatre (and, indeed, in theatre everywhere). I sincerely hope this will encourage theatre training colleges in Ireland to remove the barriers and open their doors to aspiring disabled actors. I would also urge producers to give disabled actors the support and opportunities they deserve. Not only does this advance the cause of inclusion, equality and diversity, but it creates the potential for authentic representation when a disabled performer is invited to bring their lived experience of disability to the stage or indeed to the screen. I applaud Paddy, Sorcha, Peter and Ferdia for taking on these roles and I wish them every success.

I was a long-time friend of Martin, who was an exceptional leader advancing the human rights of disabled people in Ireland, Europe and the US. A story inspired by his life will motivate others to recognise the importance of fighting for our rights as disabled people. His vision is one that enables non-disabled and disabled people to understand the changes that our communities continue to fight for to ensure equality and freedom for disabled people.

Martin Naughton was a leader and a visionary. I hope that many learn from and emulate his vision in their daily endeavours. I am proud to support *No Magic Pill* and send my best wishes for the production.

Sincerely,

Judith E. Heumann, Washington, DC

Judy Heumann was one of the main subjects of the Oscar-nominated documentary *Crip Camp*, which traces the emergence of the disability rights movement in the US in the 1970s and was executive produced by Barack and Michelle Obama for Netflix. Heumann helped to bring about the Americans with Disabilities Act in 1990 and during her career Heumann has served at the World Bank and in the Clinton administration. President Obama appointed her to a position in the State Department as a Special Advisor on International Disability Rights (a post that was eliminated after President Trump took office). She is the author of the book *Being Heumann: An Unrepentant Memoir of a Disability Rights Activist*.

Christian O'Reilly, Writer/Producer

In 1995, I was a struggling writer who needed a job. I replied to an ad in the Dublin City University newsletter placed by an organisation I'd never heard of – the Centre for Independent Living (CIL) – for a job I couldn't get my head around: a researcher/personal assistant/ communications officer. I was invited to an interview in the Royal Dublin Hotel. A man with a beard and a fishing hat was pushed through the doors in a wheelchair with a cigarette hanging out of his mouth. 'Shake the thumb,' he said. It was my first introduction to Martin Naughton. I can't remember a thing about the interview other than he told me I was starting next week. Doing what? I wondered. He smiled and told me not to worry. The following week I was thrown head first into a conference in Jury's Hotel entitled 'Disability – Investment not Burden'. I had no idea wheelchair-users could be so angry and so militant. I had no idea they wanted to change the world. Weren't they supposed to sit quietly and watch TV all day? Not these guys.

I spent two years working for Martin. He told me CIL were the 'IRA of disability' and that our job was to 'plant bombs' and agitate for change. I was a lobbyist who knew nothing about lobbying, but Martin only saw what I could do, not what I couldn't, and because he believed in me, I started to believe in myself. He had a presence, an aura, a gravitas. He could command a meeting like a general and rule with an iron fist. When you walked into a room with him to do battle, you felt confident because you knew that he was already ten steps ahead of everybody else.

When I left CIL to pursue writing again, I realised that I wanted to tell his story. But, as a non-disabled writer, I doubted my own credentials. I shared my concerns with Martin, who replied, 'There's one reason you should tell it – because you want to'. I set out to dramatise his life as a feature film, using the introduction of a personal assistance (PA) service and the fight to keep it as a backdrop. I saw this as the War of Independence for the Irish disability movement and regarded Martin as its Michael Collins. But despite my best efforts, the movie, entitled *No Magic Pill*, changed drastically during its development and turned into a different story called *Inside I'm Dancing* – a film I love and am proud of, but which doesn't tell the story I set out to tell.

I felt like I had let him down. Martin had entrusted me to tell his story, but I hadn't succeeded and it hurt. Years later, I was considering an application to the Arts Council for funding to write a play and one of my theatre mentors, Jane Daly, asked me if there was a story I wanted to write, but had never written. I thought of *No Magic Pill*, but told her I didn't know how to write it and was afraid to tackle it in case it went wrong again. Jane told me that if I was scared to write it, I had to write it. It was the sort of thing Martin would have said.

When the Arts Council awarded me funding to write the play, I knew I had to face my demons and try again. I went back to my original screenplay with a view to adapting it, but decided I needed to start afresh. I found two interviews I had conducted with Martin. They told his story from his childhood in Spiddal through to his time in St Mary's Hospital through to his activism, the founding of CIL and the campaign for PA funding. This, I decided, would be the basis for my play. But soon after starting I got stuck. I considered picking up the phone to Martin and telling him I was finally going to tell his story – but I was too embarrassed to admit I was stuck, so I decided to wait until the play was written. He died that September. I sent a note to his family, which was read out to him as he was dying. In the note, I thanked him for all he had done for me and promised I would finish the play.

I finished a first draft and approached director Raymond Keane, who was fascinated by the story of Martin, but felt the play needed considerable development. Thanks to a bursary from the Pavilion Theatre, we workshopped it in April 2017. It was a thrilling experience, but it also showed me that the play didn't work.

Niall O'Baoill urged me to seek the support of the disability community and advised that I bring a disability consultant onto my team. I approached Peter Kearns, who bluntly – and brilliantly – explained that the script felt too much like a documentary and not enough like a play. I had written a Martin character who was too saintly, too sanitised and not like the complex, interesting and flawed man he really was. Peter encouraged me to set myself free as a writer. So I started again. Yet again.

As I allowed fictional elements to combine with true life material, I felt the play start to come to life. And while it's now more accurate to say that *No Magic Pill* is inspired by Martin, rather than a literal re-telling of his life, I hope it does a better job of celebrating who he was.

Thanks to Arts Council development funding, we workshopped the play again in 2019, having made the key decision to find disabled actors to play the parts of the disabled characters. In this respect, we were guided by the CIL slogan 'Nothing about is without us'. During this crucial development process, Peter Kearns delivered a series of illuminating disability equality theatre training workshops and drilled into us the distinction between the social and medical models of disability. We worked out of the Richmond Room in Carmichael House, the location of numerous CIL board meetings, and I like to think that the spirits, ghosts and memories of all these encounters energised our conversations.

Urged on by Michael Barker-Caven, we decided to dream big and applied for Arts Council production funding through Open Call – an arduous three-stage application process that took over a year, culminating in a presentation and interview with an international jury. Producer Mitzi D'Alton had joined our team, providing crucial know-how and strategy to complement my obsessive quest to tell this story. But we narrowly missed out on Open Call funding and when we re-applied the following year, we were unsuccessful again. It felt like we had come to the end of the road, but Bea Kelleher made it clear that the Arts Council really believed in *No Magic Pill* and encouraged us to apply for Theatre Project Award funding. And here we now are, preparing to present *No Magic Pill* to the world. It has only taken me twenty-seven years.

I am indebted to my three amigos – Raymond, Peter and Mitzi – for their unwavering and tireless support during such a lengthy application experience and beyond; to the Arts Council, for supporting *No Magic Pill* from beginning to end; to all our production partners for sticking with us throughout this long journey.

I have all kinds of fears – that no one will come to see it, that critics will hate it, that Martin's family will crucify me for taking such licence with the facts of his life. But I also have all kinds of hopes – that the production will be a line in the sand for Irish theatre, showing theatre companies that disabled Irish actors deserve to play disabled characters; that Martin Naughton will start to get the sort of recognition he deserves; that it will start a conversation within wider Irish society about the need to include disabled people not just in theatre, but in everything.

Photo by Marc O'Sullivan

Photo by Marc O'Sullivan

Photo by Marc O'Sullivan

Photo by Marc O'Sullivan

Peter Kearns, Disability-Equality Dramaturg and Disability Consultant

At a basic understanding, the role of dramaturg could be seen as a production's literary advisor and their sharing of the study of plays, musicals or operas relevant to a newly written play and its crew, such as Christian's *No Magic Pill*. It is the dramaturg's job to provide the cast and crew with vital knowledge, research and interpretation about the theatrical work in question so that they are – in turn – better equipped to inform their own particular creative jobs associated with a new production.

My role as a contemporary disability-equality dramaturg is to recognise the 'voice' of lived experience and celebrate it through production-based critique and discourse with the *No Magic Pill* team. Such social model-informed dramaturgy is all about how the 'voice' of disabled characters in *No Magic Pill* must survive in a cultural world where there are still discussions by governments, doctors, charities and the non-disabled public over disabled people's basic humanity.

I am determined that a disability-equality dramaturg is centre-stage to portrayals of whether we should be born; how we should be 'cured' or institutionalised; and when we should be euthanised. Often media, film and theatre narratives frame us as the 'right' to die device or cipher and as either evil or angelic, without the narrative option of the right to live well and be bold as brass.

Faced with non-disabled drama narratives that fluctuate between contempt, pity and inspirational 'overcoming', a disability-activist dramaturg should argue the worth of disability culture critique and discourse in Irish mainstream theatre.

Raymond Keane, Director

Sometimes the clown gods play trickster and sometimes they bestow upon us gifts. More often they do both at the same time. Christian O'Reilly's *No Magic Pill* is one and both. It has turned my world upside down. Bear with me. I say I am a clown who aspires to being a fool. An ancient image depicts the fool naked from the waist down, their nakedness a sign that the true fool is prepared to show those things others prefer to hide. It is also said that the way of the fool is the wrong way which is the right way. In circus tradition the clown is the only player allowed to step outside the ring. They are, at once, outsider and insider. They are disrupters, rule breakers, havoc makers, contrariwise, laughers and criers, sometimes truth sayers, sometime liars. Artists often use the image of the clown as a metaphor for their role in society.

No Magic Pill is formed by Christian's close relationship with Martin Naughton and our disabled community. If I have learned anything from this disabled community, it is that they have little respect for the rules society imposes. They are by nature rule breakers, disruptors, havoc makers, fun makers, truth sayers, confounders as well as sowers and growers of love and humanity. This project has made me a better person, artist, clown and fool. I have found a new tribe. Come join us.

Mitzi D'Alton, Producer

As a producer, what do we look for when choosing the next project? Hopefully, a story we can be passionate about and one which offers challenge in its telling. In *No Magic Pill* we find a story about passion, about challenge, about defiance, about life – a story that demands we tell it.

This story also has another demand – to be told by and to people with lived experience of disability.

From the *social model* we learn the challenges of disability are not imposed by an impairment or condition but by a society that fails to meet the needs of a person. So our production is one of learning – we learn about the disabilities society presents, we learn about the challenges of bringing disabled people to the stage, of bringing disabled people (truly) into the auditorium.

As a producer then, we meet challenges on both sides of the curtain and learn a fact already known to those with lived experience of disability – the presence of a ramp does not mean a space *is* accessible.

To tell this story, how it wants to be told, to everybody who wants to hear it, we gather together a community of people with lived experience, with academic knowledge, with passion, with desires to learn, to create, to communicate. To this we add partners ready to take risks, to meet the challenges of disability, of language, of physical spaces, to push our views of disability in Irish theatre. And we do this not out of virtue but because we have a story worth telling, a story worth telling on its terms not ours.

No Magic Pill and Modelling a 'Cure'

Peter Kearns, *No Magic Pill* Disability-Equality Dramaturg

The nineteenth-century German disabled philosopher Friedrich Nietzsche argued that to name something is to determine its essence – to put a 'name' on something is to say what it 'is'. Some years after Nietzsche's death from syphilis, a sexually transmitted disease (STD), 1930s Nazis twisted his thinking around the essence of language by naming German disabled people *Dasein ohne Leben* ('existence-without-life').

2022 Irish disability lived experience discussions survive in a world where there are still power-plays by governments, doctors, charities and the non-disabled public. Ireland's non-disabled professionals and 'experts' still hold power over naming and labelling disabled people's basic humanity: whether we should be born; how we should be 'cured', stabilised or institutionalised; and when we should be offered the 'choice' of dying with dignity, or euthanised.

As *No Magic Pill*'s dramaturg, I set out an early argument in the process of developing the production that as social model-inspired artists we must challenge the use of medical model language everywhere we encounter such language as everyday 'barriers' to power.

Challenging the 'medical model's approach of the person with the impairment being the centre of the problem, disabled people have turned everything topsy-turvy by recognising society as the creator of disabilities. Being disabled is no longer to do with clinical labels such as cerebral palsy, multiple sclerosis, schizophrenia, AIDS, etc. *Disability* is the barriers, physical and attitudinal, developed by society that stop or restrict people with impairments. So, disabled people are not labelled by their clinical condition, but are disabled by inaccessible busses, buildings, segregated education and negative media representations. It is no longer the disabled person who *can't* get up the stairs or *can't* get on a bus; disability is created by the lack of a lift or accessible buses or *disabling* people's attitudes.

This approach includes taking to task non-disabled, and even some disabled, people who like to 'spout' the so-called politically correct terminology of 'people with disabilities' (PwD). Such medical model language continues to remove us from effective engagement with Irish 'power' systems and the willing-up of social and legislative policy. We are proudly saying that lived experience of disability should fundamentally not be a flippant catch-all phrase, but an official social model term emphasising rights and cultural identity by, for and with the expert-of-the-lived-experience – the 'disabled person'.

It is now widely appreciated that disabled people's organisations (DPOs), such as the national cross-impairment DPO Independent Living Movement of Ireland (ILMI), have a role to play in spreading *knowledge* of disability equality language which aims to impact and influence *power* with mainstream organisations, sectors and agencies, beyond the PwD disability specific arena. Since the creation of ILMI in 2018, DPOs have gained in confidence in using the strong, clear language of the social model to make sure that everyday mainstream services such as county councils, Education and Training Boards or the Health Service Executive are using such language when engaging with disabled people in every Republic of Ireland county. The 'politics' of writing social model language into mainstream social agencies and their policy is about two things: social organisation and power. Disability equality activists cannot get away with ignoring medical model language like 'people with disabilities' when engaging mainstream organisations, even if we want to. Understanding the critical difference between the two terms 'disabled person' and 'PwD' allows us to talk separately and clearly about:

- a named individual = the person
- impairment = their 'expert' understanding of how their body functions
- disability = society's physical and attitudinal barriers and obsession with the personal-tragedy story and non-disabled professional perceived health-deviancy 'cure'.

Unfortunately, too many non-disabled disability-sector staff, health workers and social workers still insist on using the medical model 'PwD', i.e. the impairment and the individual being the disabling 'problem' to be fixed. Such mistaken political correctness around disability terminology can simply confuse issues, by advocating terms such as physically challenged, visually challenged, mentally challenged, etc. Such expressions detract from the real disabling issues: such as those that are being challenged by *No Magic Pill*'s production.

Disabled people have no problem with their difference. It can be good craic, but we do feel challenged by other people's lack of tolerance and by the barriers that make it harder for us to participate. So, although disabled people have impairments, they are disabled by outside forces that oppress them daily, including shape-shifting 'labels' imposed on individuals.

The term 'disabled person' has become positive and empowering, as it denotes the recognition of oppression and affiliation to a movement, such as an Irish DPO like ILMI. Used as a verb – I am disabled by attitudes; she is disabled by systems, he faces disabling structures – recognises disability as a social oppression, something external to the person. Significantly, it also acknowledges that 'disability' can be changed and transformed by collective activists in social model-led DPOs.

Disabled activists use the term 'impairment' to talk about their medical condition or diagnosis or description of their bodily functioning. Activists also use the term 'perceived impairments', which identifies that impairment 'labels' constantly change meaning according to the medical fad of the day. Being born in the 1960s, I was then clinically labelled 'spastic'. Now the label is 'cerebral palsy'. I have no control over such clinical label shape-shifting, but I can promote social model language, although a lot of people still see me as a bit of a 'spa'! So, impairment clinical names are label shape-shifters, usually dictated by the medical and health policy community, and can be just names for a list of medical model-led subjective health-deviant language such as bodily appearances. The shape-shifting impairment label language can overshadow the individual. By its nature, impairment label language can't recognise the strong impact of a disabled person's class, gender, ethnic background, etc. on their life course (birth to death) lived experiences.

Faced with powerful, non-disabled medical model language and narratives that fluctuate between basic existence, contempt, pity and 'super crip' or inspirational 'overcoming', how should we of *No Magic Pill*'s team argue the worth of social model rights, culture, critique and discourse in the Irish lived experience of disability on Irish mainstream theatre stages? Often Irish theatre and cultural narratives frame the lived experience of disability as a lifetime of 'problems', of 'cures' and peddling the 'right' to die, without the option of the right to live and celebrate disabled people's life course experiences, as with *No Magic Pill*'s characters.

A social model-informed communication of the lived experience, such as that of *No Magic Pill*'s production approach, could be seen to be breaking through the idea, presented to disabled people by some of the medical profession and disability charities in particular, that their situations are different and unrelated. As with the collective struggle of characters in *No Magic Pill*, under the social model lived experience, disabled people come together not as the blind or the deaf or the epileptic, or the bipolars, or the spastic or the arthritic impairment-based groupings, but as disabled people and activists and body-owning corporeal-cultural enablers who also have important stories of class, gender, ethnicity, sexual orientation, etc.

Collectivism of language and power and disability activism is very much about being visible and troublesome . . . and controversial, with political themes and usually sexually charged imagery and narratives harvested from the lived experience. Since the establishment of ILMI in 2018, Irish DPOs' main thrust with disability activism and the lived experience is to capacity build and ensure that disabled people explore identity and speak up and out for themselves – to themselves.

The way we use language, such as the social model term *disabled people*, in the lived experience of disability can only encourage rights, cultural, political and identity transformation. It is an important part of the narrative-way that together we construct shared lived experience understandings and expectations about disabled people and the way we relate to and improve what it is to be human.

In Memory of

Martin Naughton

Dermot Walsh

Ursula Hagerty

Florence Dougall

Hubert McCormack

Joe T. Mooney

Jana Overbo

John Doyle

Gordana Rajkov

Donal Toolan

Dennis O'Brien

Declan O'Keeffe

Michael Corbett

Eugene Callan

Brian Malone

James Brosnan

Dr John Roche

Aaron Abbey

Cathal Philbin

Frank Larkin

Biographies

Christian O'Reilly – Writer/Producer

Christian is an award-winning playwright and screenwriter based in Galway.

Christian's plays include *It Just Came Out* (Druid Debut Series, 2001), *The Good Father* (Druid – Galway Arts Festival 2002; national tour 2003; joint winner of the 2002 Stewart Parker Trust New Playwright Bursary), *Is This About Sex?* (Rough Magic – 2007 Edinburgh Fringe Festival; 50th Dublin Theatre Festival; winner of Best Theatre Script at the 2008 Irish Writers' Guild Awards), *Here We Are Again Still* (Decadent/Galway City Council – 2009 Nun's Island; Bealtaine Festival and national tour in 2011), *Sanctuary* (Blue Teapot – 2012 Galway Theatre Festival; 2013 Galway Arts Festival and Dublin Fringe Festival) and *Chapatti* (Northlight/Galway International Arts Festival, 2014; nominated for Best New Work at the 2014 Jeff Awards, which celebrate excellence in Chicago theatre).

A graduate of the 2011 BBC Writers' Academy, his screen credits include episodes of *Doctors*, *Casualty*, *Holby City* (all BBC One), *On Home Ground* (RTE), *Deception* (TV3) and *Red Rock* (TV3); three short films (*The Kiss of Life*, *The Birthday* and *The Ring*); and *Inside I'm Dancing*, a feature film based on his original story. *Inside I'm Dancing* won the Audience Award for Best Film at the Edinburgh Film Festival (2004) and two Irish Film and Television Awards – Best Script (2004) and Best Irish Film (2005). It was released in the United States as *Rory O'Shea Was Here*.

Christian's screen adaptation of his play *Sanctuary* received its world premiere at the Galway Film Fleadh in July 2016, winning the award for Best First Irish Feature. He is currently in his second year as playwright-in-residence at the Town Hall Theatre, Galway, a role he also held during 2011 and 2012.

Sorcha Curley – Ursula

Sorcha Curley is a graduate of the Gaiety School of Acting at the National Theatre School of Ireland where she studied Performance and Advanced Performance Year.

Productions performed at the Gaiety included: *Portia Coughlan* by Marina Carr, *Tea in a China Cup* by Christina Reid and *Love's Labour's Lost* by William Shakespeare.

Most recently Sorcha appeared in her second short film *Try and Touch* by Nell Henesey, Funded for Films in Limerick and Engine Shorts Film Scheme.

Mark Fitzgerald – Brendan/Minister/Doctor/Physio Two/Vinny/Max

Mark Fitzgerald recently appeared in *Happy Birthday Dear Alice* and *The Beauty Queen of Leenane* produced by FourRivers Theatre Company, Walls and Windows and Abbey Calling, and *The Plough and the Stars* produced by the Abbey Theatre. He performed in the remount tour of Verdant Productions' *A Holy Show* and has been in several productions for Second Age, including *Macbeth* and *Romeo and Juliet*, as well as playing Hamlet.

Mark trained at the Drama Centre London and at Ecole Philippe Gaulier in Paris.

Film/TV credits include: *Recently Appeared in Valhalla* (Netflix), *The Northman*, *Little Women* (BBC), *Muse* (Fantastic Films), *My Mother and Other Strangers* (BBC), *Vikings* (MGM) and *Loving Miss Hatto* (BBC).

Theatre credits include: *Copperface Jacks: The Musical* (Olympia Theatre), *Alone it Stands* (Verdant), *Luck Just Kissed You Hello* (GIAF/Dublin Theatre Festival) and *Break* (Hot for Theatre), *Still, the Blackbird Sings* (Derry Playhouse), *A Midsummer Night's Dream* (Storytellers Theatre Company), *Bacchaefull* (Dirty Market), *Too Much Punch for Judy* (Ape Theatre Company), *A Harlot's Progress* (Tightrope), *Cruel and Tender* (Project Arts Centre), *Oedipus Rex* (Company of Angels), *Duck* (Edinburgh Fringe Festival), *Romeo and Juliet* (Gaiety Theatre) *Foxy* (Project Arts Centre) and *On the Other Side of the Wall* (UK/Algeria Tour)

Peter Kearns – Dermot/Disability-Equality Dramaturg and Disability Consultant

Coolock native Peter Kearns escaped a southside Dublin special school in the mid-1970s and currently works with the Independent Living Movement Ireland (ILMI.ie) as their Leitrim-based cross-border social inclusion project coordinator and dramatist/disability-equality mentor. Peter graduated from Trinity College Dublin in the late 1980s with an Hons. English Degree and followed this with an MA in Film & TV Studies at Dublin City University and a Higher Diploma in Adult & Community Education from Maynooth College. He also has Higher Diplomas in Disability Studies and Arts European Mentoring. Since the noughties, Peter has been a lecturer at St Angela's College, Sligo (ATU), and has written up many QQI-Level 8 & 9 Modules promoting a need for an emancipatory-advocacy way of thinking and practice for and with disabled people.

As Development & Policy Worker with the Forum of People with Disabilities, Peter worked in New York in the early noughties at the United Nations on developing disabled people's organisation (DPO) community development inputs into the 2007 UN Convention on the Rights of Disabled People. After some years as Dublin City Arts Centre Education Director, in the late 1990s, Peter established The Workhouse, a disability consultancy company involved in disability-equality/mentor/arts training in Ireland, Europe and Asia.

Peter's associate residency at the Abbey Theatre (2000–3) facilitated the development of a disability access policy and promoted a vision for the National Cultural Institutions' beginning of an ongoing relationship with disabled people as audience, creators and producers. Since leaving the Abbey Theatre, he has produced and directed a series of touring adult cabaret shows with disabled performers. Critically recognised drama work has included Cork Year of Culture establishment of Forum Theatre groups at Cork Cheshire Homes, Firestation Artists Studio disability arts website, Dundalk Disability Forum Theatre and Dublin/Sligo/Galway Disability & Forum Theatre groups.

Peter has also directed and produced a number of broadcast videos, such as *Wetting Our Saris*, a UN half-hour documentary on anti-poverty projects in western Bangladesh, and a Centre for Independent Living half-hour training documentary. With disabled students from the EU Horizon Lights-Disability-Action, he has produced a number of film festival shorts such as *A View to a Job*, *Lead Us Not*, *The Spa*, *Cabaret Freaks* and *Art Intervention* – shown and receiving awards at festivals such as Galway Film Fleadh, Berlin, London, and San Francisco. Peter is currently producing a series of social media videos and activist filmed portraits with ILMI.

Peter is Chairperson of Glens Arts Centre Manorhamilton, Co. Leitrim. He is married to Teresa and has two 'adult' children, Deirbhile and Oisin.

Ferdia MacAonghasa – Mick/Albert/Sean

Ferdia graduated in 2019 from the National Film School of Ireland, winning the Aileen McKeogh award for contributing 'most in practice and principle to the vision of Arts'.

His debut feature screenplay *Briefly Gorgeous* is in development with Screen Ireland and Pale Rebel Productions.

He writes stories for RTÉ's long-running soap opera *Fair City* and has published a number of columns in the *Irish Times*.

A commenter on the IT website named Steve once accused him of fighting against 'everything the enlightenment, free speech and the scientific method stand for'. He's unreasonably proud of this – he thinks it makes him sound much cooler than he actually is.

No Magic Pill is his professional acting debut.

Julie Sharkey – Josie/Mother/Physio One/Sister

Julie Sharkey is from Ballaghaderreen in Co. Roscommon and is a graduate of the Gaiety School of Acting. She holds a Diploma in Drama in Education and an MA in Drama and Theatre Studies from University College Cork. Recent theatre credits include: the new folk musical *In the Midst of Plenty* by Amy Day for Enchanted Croí Theatre, performed at the National Famine Museum at Strokestown Park House; *The Three Fat Women of Antibes* by W. Somerset Maugham performed at King House Boyle as part of the Local Live Performance Scheme 2022; and *Alice and the Wolf* by Tom Swift, national tour for Barnstorm in Kilkenny. As a writer Julie's children's play *An Ant Called Amy* was filmed and presented as part of Cruinniú na nÓg 2021 and will embark on a national tour in autumn 2022, a co-production with Roscommon Arts Centre with Raymond Keane directing. A recipient of an Arts Council Agility Award, Julie is currently collaborating with an ex-showband member and nursing home resident developing a one-woman play based on showband music. Film/TV work include *The Last Right*, *Mammal*, *The Runway*, *Death of a Superhero*, *32A*, *Situations Vacant*, *Fair City*, *Red Rock*, *Smalltown* and *The Clinic*. As drama facilitator Julie works extensively in Arts and Health and

Education working with the Health Service Executive, Daughters of Charity, St Michael's House, Creative Schools and Artist in Schools Programmes.

Paddy Slattery – Martin

Paddy Slattery is a multi-IFTA-nominated filmmaker who fell in love with filmmaking during an uncertain time in his life, following a serious car accident. He subsequently remains quadriplegic but, in Paddy's words, 'My body switched off and my imagination switched on'.

Paddy recently wrote, directed and produced his debut film and his work has collectively screened at over 100 film festivals worldwide, been broadcast on Sky Arts and RTE 2, and picked up over forty awards including two Royal Television Society Awards and a John Boorman Special Achievement Award presented by the multi-Oscar-nominated filmmaker himself.

Paddy's debut feature *Broken Law*, which received completion funding from Screen Ireland, had its world premiere at VMDIFF20 in front of a sold-out crowd in the IMAX and went on to win a Special Jury Prize by the Dublin Film Critics' Circle along with an Aer Lingus Discovery Award. *Broken Law* was released in cinemas nationwide and became the highest-grossing Irish film of 2020 before its Netflix release in Ireland and UK where it went straight in at no. 2 in the movie charts of that week.

www.standmantra.com

Raymond Keane – Director

Raymond is a founding member of multi-award-winning Barabbas Theatre Company. www.barabbas.ie.

Raymond's work as clown, actor, writer and director has appeared in almost every Irish theatre and on international stages from the back of a truck to the Brooklyn Academy of Music – London, Edinburgh, Wales, France, Denmark, Africa (Zimbabwe and Zambia), Japan, New Zealand and the United States (New York, Washington, Kansas, Chicago, New Hampshire, Colorado and Connecticut).

He has collaborated with Sarah Jane Scaife (Company SJ) on her *Beckett in the City* project that continues to tour nationally and internationally. So far, this work has been presented at Dublin Theatre

Festival, Dublin Fringe Festival, Cork Midsummer Festival, Enniskillen and Paris Beckett Festivals, Barbican Beckett Festival in London, River to River Festival in New York and Tokyo.

Most recent performances include Beckett's short novel *Company* directed by Sarah Jane Scaife at Dublin Theatre Festival in 2018, *Ulysses* at the Abbey Theatre in 2018 and 2019, Theatre Lovett/Irish National Opera/Abbey Theatre's production of *Hansel & Gretel*, winner Best Opera and nominated Best Lighting Design (Sarah Jane Shiels), Irish Times Theatre Awards 2022. *Laethanta Sona* (*Happy Days*) by Samuel Beckett with Bríd Ní Neachtain as Winnie under the direction of Sarah Jane Scaife – Company SJ performed on Inis Óir and at Dublin Theatre Festival in October 2021. Bríd won Best Actress ITTA 2022 and Ger Clancy was nominated for Best Design.

Most recent directing includes the award-winning *How to Square a Circle* at Dublin Fringe Festival and subsequent national tour, *More Rope* by Billy Roche for Abbey Theatre's 14 Voices from a Bloodied Field, *NASC* for Infinite Pants Co. *The Long Christmas Dinner* (Abbey/Peacock Stage) was nominated in five categories at the 2022 Irish Times Theatre Awards: Best Director; Best Production; Best Ensemble; Best Supporting Actor, Máire Ní Ghráinne; and (winner of) Best Lighting Design, Stephen Dodd.

He is a performer in John Gerard's *Mirrored Pavilion* – Galway International Arts Festival.

Film and television appearances include *Fair City*, *The Boy from Mercury*, *St Patrick*, *Bloom*, *Sweety Barrett*, *The Lonely Battle of Thomas Reid*, *Procession*, *To the Moon* and *Game of Thrones.*

He teaches Theatre of Clown at Gaiety School of Acting Dublin, The Lir Academy of Dramatic Arts Dublin and The Samuel Beckett School of Dramatic Arts Trinity College Dublin – where he is Adjunct Teaching Fellow. He regularly mentors theatre artists.

Ger Clancy – Set Designer

Ger Clancy is the creative director of ArtFX, an art studio based in Wicklow, Ireland. With over twenty years' experience in the arts, he works as a designer, artist and educator.

He is actively involved in theatre, film, spectacle and visual arts. He is programme chair of the Design for Film course at the Institute of Art,

Design and Technology, Dun Laoghaire. He has lectured there since 2003.

Ger is a determined, creative individual who enjoys the challenge of creating new work. Always striving to achieve superior innovative solutions, he is keen to ensure that his designs and artwork leave a lasting impression on audiences.

Sarah Jane Shiels – Lighting Designer

Sarah Jane Shiels began designing lighting in Dublin Youth Theatre, completing an MSc in Interactive Digital Media in 2021, a BA in Drama and Theatre Studies in 2006 (Trinity) and the Rough Magic Seeds3 programme 2006–8. During 2010–17, she was co-artistic director of WillFredd Theatre.

Recent lighting designs include *Party Scene*, *SHIT*, *Conversations After Sex* (This Is Pop Baby), *The Tin Soldier* (Theatre Lovett, The Gate), *All the Angels* (Rough Magic Theatre Company), *Book of Names* (ANU Productions), *The Veiled Ones* (Junk Ensemble), *Afterlove* (Stephanie Dufresne, Galway Dance Project), *Luck Just Kissed You Hello*, *One Good Turn* (Abbey Theatre), *Hansel and Gretel* (Irish National Opera, Theatre Lovett, Abbey Theatre).

Deirdre Dwyer – Costume Designer

Deirdre Dwyer designs sets and costumes for theatre, opera, dance and film. She is also a writer, director and dramaturg. Her training includes a BA in English and Drama & Theatre Studies, University College Cork (UCC), 2004, an MA in Theatre Design, Royal Welsh College of Music & Drama, Cardiff, 2016 and apprenticing as Designer on the Rough Magic SEEDS3 programme, 2007/8.

She is a member of BrokenCrow, a multidisciplinary ensemble-led theatre company, with whom she has designed seven productions, created two shows and two audio dramas. She has been a visiting lecturer, teaching design and related theories, to students at UCC, Mary Immaculate College, Limerick (where she was Theatre Artist in Residence in 2017–20), Institute of Art, Design and Technology, Dublin and South East Technological University. She is a founder member of the Irish Society for Stage and Screen Design (ISSSD), and chairperson of the ISSSD's Prague Quadrennial Subcommittee, organising the Irish Entry for PQ2023.

She has previously designed for companies including the Everyman, London Academy of Music & Dramatic Art, Royal Conservatoire Scotland, Graffiti, Royal Welsh College of Music & Drama, Rough Magic, Little Red Kettle, Junk Ensemble, Graffiti and Cork Opera House.

She has been Theatre Artist in Residence at Garter Lane Arts Centre, Waterford, since 2020.

www.deirdredwyer.com

Trevor Knight – Composer and Sound Designer

Trevor Knight is a composer/director/actor who specialises in multidisciplinary and collaborative work.

He was a keyboard player in 1970s with Irish bands Naima and Metropolis. In 1980 in Holland he formed Auto da Fé with singer Gay Woods. They recorded three albums – *Tatitum*, *Five Singles and One Smoked Cod* and *Gazette* – touring Ireland and the UK extensively. In 2001 a live BBC session, *Songs for Echo*, was released and a double CD compilation, *When the Curtain Goes Bang! An Anthology*, was released in 2020.

He has recorded and performed with artists such as Phil Lynott, Donovan, Paul Brady, Honor Heffernan, Mary Coughlan, Those Nervous Animals and Roger Doyle.

He has written more than seventy scores for theatre including *Catalpa* (Donal O'Kelly), which has toured the world and won an Edinburgh Fringe First), *Juno and the Paycock* (The Abbey) and *Circus* for Barabbas.

As theatre director/composer, work includes *Bleeding Poets*, *Just a Little One – A Dorothy Parker Cocktail* and *The Whistling Girl* (musical settings of the poetry of Dorothy Parker) with vocalist Honor Heffernan. The show toured Ireland, as well as Belgrade and New York, and a CD was released in 2017.

He composed the music for, conceived and directed *slat* (2007), *The Devils Spine Band* (2011), *The Gift*, *Visitant* (2014), all featuring Japanese Butoh dancers Maki Watanabe and Gyohei Zaitsu and a variety of musicians, dancers and performers over the years. A CD of DSB music will be released later this year.

Film soundtracks include *Double Carpet* (Channel 4), *What Am I Doing Here* and *Rough Time* (dir. Trish MacAdam), and for RADE the shorts *Spare Change* and *The Tappers Opera*.

Many collaborations with visual artist Alice Maher include *The Music of Things*, *Godchildren of Enantios* (Dublin, London and New York) and *Cassandra's Necklace* (IMMA, Dublin, 2012).

He has been a member of Aosdana since 2007.

Rachel Parry – Movement Director

Rachel Parry is originally from North Wales and works from Galway as a choreographer, dance facilitator and third-level teacher. She trained in dance at Bretton Hall College (Leeds) and at the Hogeschool for the Kunsten (Arnhem, Netherlands). Rachel is artistic director of Speckled Egg Dance Company (Galway). She is currently studying for a PhD in Drama, Theatre and Performance at National University of Ireland Galway.

Andrea Ainsworth – Voice Coach

Andrea Ainsworth is one of the foremost voice specialists in Ireland. She has been the Voice Director of the Abbey Theatre since 1995, working closely with both Irish and international directors on all productions in the Abbey and Peacock Theatres including premieres of plays by Seamus Heaney, Tom Murphy, Frank McGuiness, Marina Carr, Conor McPherson and Tom Kilroy. She has taught in drama schools in London and was a lecturer in Voice and Text in the School of Drama, Trinity College Dublin from 1995 until 2008. She has worked with many of the independent theatre companies in Ireland – most recently with director Yaël Farber on *Hamlet* at the Gate Theatre and St. Ann's Warehouse in Brooklyn, New York. For the Peacock Theatre, she has adapted and directed storytelling plays by Marina Carr, Paula Meehan and Éilís Ní Dhuibhne and also directed a series of poetry cabarets with singers and actors. Recent directing work includes *Every Brilliant Thing* with Amy Conroy at the Peacock and touring.

At the Abbey, she offers classes and bespoke voice workshops for a variety of groups including actors, teachers, lobbyists, business clients, writers and lecturers. She has designed and delivered a series of workshops for teachers on Shakespeare.

She also coaches actors for film and TV.

Hillary Dziminski – Marketing Manager

Hillary Dziminski is a creative producer and marketing manager working across theatre, film and live events. She holds an MA in Drama & Performance Studies from University College Dublin and an MFA in Playwriting from The Lir Academy at Trinity College Dublin. She is the lead producer for Pan Platform and an associate producer for Bewley's Cafe Theatre. She is currently based between Dublin and Florence.

Marie Tierney – Production Manager

Marie Tierney works both as a designer and production manager for theatre and film.

As a production manager, she has toured extensively both nationally and internationally. Recent production management credits include *Our Little World* in Mud Island community garden, *Julius Caesar* for TU Drama and *Duck Goose*, *The Alternative*, *Haughey Gregory*, *On Blueberry Hill* and *Rathmines Road* for Fishamble the New Play Company

She has coordinated many large-scale and site-specific productions. Previously she has been design coordinator on many productions such as St Patrick's Festival, a number of site-specific shows in swimming pools with Big Telly and shows in Kilmainham Gaol.

She has a particular interest in working in the community and is currently a member of the steering committee for the Creative Arts project in Darndale.

As a film designer, she designed costumes for *Borstal Boy*, *Mapmaker*, *Crushproof*, *The Disappearance of Finbar*, *On Home Ground* for RTÉ and many Filmbase shorts. She designed set and costumes for Kathleen Lynn's *The Rebel Doctor* and James Gandon's *A Life for Loopline* films.

She is a coordinator in Colaiste Dhulaigh's Performing Arts Department and she delivers modules in technical theatre and design. She holds a Master's Degree in Theatre Practice.

She is a member of the board of directors of Axis Arts in Ballymun and the Association of Irish Stage Technicians, which promotes safety and training in the arts.

Donna Leonard – Stage Manager

Donna Leonard has worked as a stage manager for many years in an array of Irish theatres as well in London's West End and across the UK. Shows to date include numerous pantomimes at the Gaiety Theatre; *The Snapper*, *Little Women*, *Death of a Salesman*, *The Father*, *Our New Girl*, *My Cousin Rachel*, *Tribes*, *Threepenny Opera* at the Gate Theatre; *Singing in the Rain*, *The Walworth Farce*, *Once the Musical* at The Olympia, Dublin; *Drum Belly*, *Heartbreak House*, *The Risen People* at the Abbey Theatre. West End shows include *Fiddler on the Roof*, *The King and I*, *High Society*, *An Ideal Husband* and *Jesus Christ Superstar* among many others.

Róisín Ní Ghabhann – Assistant Stage Manager

Róisín Ní Ghabhann holds a Bachelor's Degree in Costume Design from the Institute of Art, Design and Technology, Dún Laoghaire. Her main area of work in film and theatre is as a costume technician. Recent credits include *The Clean Up Crew* and *The Last Girl* (Hail Mary Pictures). For No Magic Pill, Róisín's role is assistant stage manager.

Mitzi D'Alton – Producer

Mitzi D'Alton is a cultural producer with twelve years' experience within theatre, festivals, events and cultural community projects in Dublin. She holds a BA in Arts Management from IADT, Dún Laoghaire. Mitzi has worked in a variety of roles with an array of arts and cultural organisations including Helium Arts, Science Gallery Dublin, Dublin Theatre Festival, Dublin's Culture Connects, National Gallery of Ireland, The Ark, Dublin Fringe Festival and Dublin City Council led festivals, alongside independent freelance projects.

Recent theatre productions include Emily Aoibheann's *Mother of Pearl*, and *Sorry Gold* at Project Arts Centre, Dublin Fringe Festival 2019; Little Lion Dance Theatre's *A-do-le-TA!*; the award-winning *The Woods & Grandma* by Dead Lady Productions, Dublin Fringe Festival 2017, *Hostel16* by Fionnuala Gygax, Dublin Fringe Festival 2016; the award-winning *Object Piggy* by Emily Aoibheann, Dublin Fringe Festival 2015; and *Stefan Fae's Cabaret Mattachine*, Dublin Fringe Festival 2014, amongst others.

Photo by Kamyla Abreu

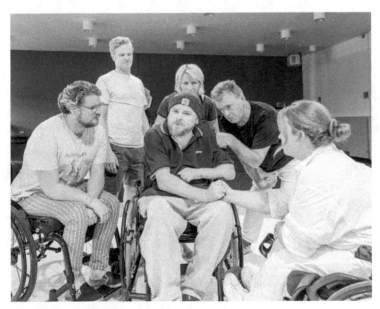

Photo by Kamyla Abreu

Photo by Kamyla Abreu

Photo by Kamyla Abreu

Special Thanks

The Arts Council of Ireland – Bea Kelleher, Karl Wallace, David Parnell and all the staff at the Arts Council.

Our partners – Damien Walshe, Nina Byrne, James Cawley and all at Independent Living Movement Ireland; Joan Carthy and all at Irish Wheelchair Association; John Dolan, Gary Lee, Allen Dunne, Martina Nicholson and all at Disability Federation of Ireland; Sandra Doyle, Niamh Honer, Dermot Marrey, Donal Shiels and all at The Civic, Tallaght; Fergal McGrath and all at the Town Hall Theatre and Black Box; Gary McMahon and all at Galway City Council; Sharon O'Grady, Amie Lawless and all at Galway County Council; Ray Yeates and all at Dublin City Council; Selina Bonnie and Orla Scannell and all at South Dublin County Council; Willie White and all at Dublin Theatre Festival.

International supporters – Judy Heumann; Adolf Ratzka; John Evans; Baroness Jane Campbell; Ger Quinn.

Irish supporters – Jane Daly; Ailbhe Slevin, Cóilín O'Reilly and Fia O'Reilly; Michael Barker-Caven; Barbara Naughton and Martin Naughton's family; Rosaleen McDonagh; Feilim O'hAoláin; Rhona Coughlan; James Harrold; Padraig Naughton and all at Arts & Disability Ireland; Tríona Ní Dhuibhir; Maria Fleming; Joe Flavin; Niall O'Baoill; Joanna Marsden; John Given; James Flynn and Juanita Wilson; Eamon Howley; Mark O'Brien and Caitriona McLaughlin of the Abbey Theatre; Stefan Lundstrom, The Galmont Hotel & Spa; Nathaniel Tracey, Nothingless Photography; Marc, Joanne and Niamh at Branar; Jean and Síomha at Druid; Daryl McCormack; Bernie Slevin; Teresa, Deirbhile and Oisin Kearns; Cora Doyle and all at Artane School of Music; Harry Giles; all the staff at Carmichael House; Senator Erin McGreehan; Anne Rabitte, TD, Minister of State at the Department of Children, Equality, Disability, Integration and Youth and at the Department of Health.

Dom, Sam, Ian and all at Methuen Drama.

BLACK BOX THEATRE

 Comhairle Cathrach
Bhaile Átha Cliath
Dublin City Council

Comhairle Cathrach na Gaillimhe
Galway City Council

Comhairle Chontae na Gaillimhe
Galway County Council

No Magic Pill

Characters

Martin
Josie
Ursula
Dermot
Mick
Minister
Brendan
Mother
Doctor
Physio One
Physio Two
Vinny
Sister
Albert
Sean
Max

Scene One

June 1994. The viewing gallery of Dáil Éireann. **Martin, Josie, Ursula, Dermot** *and* **Mick** *eyeball the Minister for Health.* **Martin** *is confident to the point of smug; the others are anxious.*

Minister   We welcome members of the Centre for Independent Living to our chambers this evening. Indeed, we welcome the very emergence of this group in Irish society and support its slogan, 'Nothing about us about without us'. The rights of Irish people with disabilities have long been ignored, but the rights of severely disabled Irish people even more so. The success of the two-year, EU-funded pilot programme of personal assistance under the Horizon scheme cannot be denied. The lives of twenty-nine disabled have been transformed for the better. They have left family homes and institutions and lives of passive dependency to embrace opportunities to study, work, travel, to participate equally as members of Irish society. They are an example to us all.

Martin (*to his friends*)   So far so good.

Minister   And they have come to us today, to the gates of the Irish Parliament, to ask for a continuation of the lives they have only just begun. The reality, however, is that it was crystal clear from the outset that this European-funded programme was limited to two years. In addition, I am troubled to be made aware of a level of financial mismanagement that suggests an inability to cope with a budget of this size. I have great sympathy for this group of people, but the government simply cannot be held to ransom like this. And so it is with regret that my department must decline its request for financial assistance.

A long silence. Everyone is shocked and devastated. He stares in disbelief.

Martin   No. No. Noooooouuuuuoooooo!

His friends withdraw in silence. **Martin** *sits in his wheelchair, alone and in the depths of despair.*

For the scenes that take place in the present, **Martin** *will be* **Martin P** *(for Present) and* **Brendan** *will be* **Brendan P**.

Martin P   Come on, Martin. Think! Think! Come on, come on, come on. You can do this. You can do this.

Brendan *appears behind* **Martin**, *slowly wheeling his chair.*

Martin P   Brendan? Where did you come out of?

Brendan P   How should I know? You were always the one with the answers.

Martin P   Yeah, well I don't have the answers now.

Brendan P   Do you have the questions?

Martin P   All I've got are questions.

Brendan P   So, what are the questions?

Martin P   I . . . I can't. I don't have time. There's too much to explain.

Brendan P   Try me.

Martin P   I don't have time, I said. I need to work out and decide. I always . . . I always know what to do.

Brendan P   What do you need to work out and decide? I'm great at that sort of thing.

Martin P   Look, leave me alone, will you? I need to think. They depend on me.

Brendan P   Who depends on you?

Martin P   Just leave me alone.

Brendan P   Grand so.

He starts to leave.

Martin P   Wait! Wait.

Brendan P *returns.*

Martin P   It's just . . . it's been so long . . .

Brendan P   You've missed me.

Martin P   I wouldn't go that far.

Brendan P   Deny it all you want. I know deep down it's true.

Martin P   Fuck off so.

Brendan P   Do you remember how we met?

Martin P   How we met? Who cares how we met?

Brendan P   It might help you work out what to do.

Martin P   No, I'm not doing that. I don't need your help.

Brendan P   Ah, Martin. I just want to know what happened to you. Please.

Scene Two

1962. Spiddal. **Martin**'*s mother and* **Doctor** *watch as* **Martin** *(nine) tries to walk on crutches.*

Brendan P   Wait a minute – where are we? This isn't St Mary's.

Martin P   Do you want to hear my story or not?

Brendan P   Yeah, the cool bits. The bits with me in it.

Martin P   Do you not recognise that fella?

They watch young **Martin** *as he tries to walk.*

Mother   That's it, Martin, keep going. You're doing well.

The strain is too much. **Martin** *collapses. His mother and the* **Doctor** *help him up.*

Mother   That's fine, Martin. Well done.

Martin   Sorry, Mam. My arms are just too tired.

Mother   It's okay.

She sits **Martin** *on a chair. She and the* **Doctor** *talk in private.*

Mother   Is there a small improvement maybe?

Doctor   Does he get enough to eat, do you think?

Mother   Enough to eat?

Doctor   Only you've six mouths to feed and he wouldn't be the quickest to the table.

Mother   He never goes hungry, if that's what you're asking.

Doctor   I'm just trying to understand why he's not thriving. He's how old now?

Mother   He's nine.

Doctor   It's strange. He could walk for years. Until he was six?

Mother   Did he catch something maybe? A virus?

Doctor   I've never seen it before. I wonder was it an insect bite?

Mother   Should I try another priest?

Doctor   Was the last one any good?

Mother   He had the cure for ringworm only. And he didn't even have that.

Doctor   Did Lourdes help at all?

Mother   He came back clean anyway. They bathed him in holy water for a week.

Doctor   Have you thought any more about that place in Dublin?

Mother   I'm not sending him away.

Doctor   He's not getting better. If anything –

Mother   This is his home. His sisters and brother – they play with him. It's almost as if they can't play without him. They push him 'round on a bicycle. He's always at the centre of things.

Doctor   If you want him to be able to walk . . .

Mother   But what's wrong with him?

Doctor   The Little Willie has a great record with polio patients.

Mother   The little what?

Doctor   St Mary's Hospital in Baldoyle. They call it the Little Willie. It's named after a young fella that had polio.

Mother   But is that what this is? Polio?

The **Doctor** *doesn't know. He leaves.* **Mother** *turns to* **Martin**.

Mother   You'll see us at Christmas.

Martin   I don't want to go.

Mother   You won't feel the time passing.

Martin   I'll try harder.

Mother   We'll visit you when we can. You'll make friends, great friends. Think of it as an adventure.

Martin   Don't make me go.

Mother   We need to get you well. What's going to become of you otherwise? Now is the time to do it before it's too late. I'll collect you myself at Christmas. We'll drive back to Spiddal together and we'll get the turkey and ham on the way home. What do you think about that? Be brave, Martin. It's for the best.

She hugs him.

Scene Three

The physio department of St Mary's Hospital. **Physio One** *and* **Physio Two** *work on young* **Martin**.

Brendan P   Ah, here we are. God, I almost forgot about these two.

Martin P   Really?

Brendan P   No.

Physio One   Porridge. Every day.

Physio Two   With sugar? Jam? No – honey?

Physio One   Salt.

Physio Two   Salt? Ah no. Every day?

Physio One   For years now.

Physio Two   Do you not get sick of it?

Physio One   Never.

Physio Two   I have to have something sweet.

Physio One   Very bad for the teeth.

Physio Two   Toast and jam. My mother makes an amazing blackberry jam.

Physio One   Sometimes I like a scone.

Physio Two   Aha.

Physio One   But never in the morning. Only as a treat.

Martin   Can I have something to eat?

Physio Two   Only as a treat? But jam isn't a treat.

Physio One   It tastes even nicer when you seldom have it.

Martin   Please. Something to eat?

Physio One   What was that?

Martin   I never got any breakfast this morning.

Physio Two   That's some accent. Where's he from?

Physio One   Connemara, I think. Spiddal?

Martin   Are you from Connemara too?

Physio Two   Is that all he has – the Irish?

Physio One   Don't worry. He'll soon adjust.

Physio Two   He'll have to.

Physio One   Do you speak any English, Martin?

Martin *doesn't understand.*

Physio Two   I love a scone with my mother's jam. Delicious.

Physio One   You live well, it sounds like.

Martin   I'm hungry. I need something to eat.

Physio Two   A toasted scone. Now that's –

Martin   Why won't you listen to me?

Physio Two   You'll have to learn some English, Martin. What do you think about that?

Physio One (*to* **Martin**)   I'll get you something soon. Just be patient. Do you understand me at all?

Physio Two   And chocolate. I love chocolate.

Physio One   I'd hate to be your dentist.

Physio One *and* **Physio Two** *leave.* **Martin** *is left alone. Young* **Brendan** *appears in a wheelchair.*

Brendan   You're wasting your time.

Martin   What? You speak Irish?

Brendan   And English. I'll teach you if you want. Fuck-all else to be doing.

Martin   I don't want to learn English. I want to get out of here.

Brendan   They did the same shite with me for months. The torture chamber. The worst thing is when they forget about you and you need the jacks. You can shout and scream all you want. They won't hear you. The corridors in this place go on for miles.

Martin   You said I'm wasting my time. What do you mean?

Brendan   You're like me. A Muscie.

Martin   A what?

Brendan   I heard the doctors talking about you. Muscular dystrophy. The Polios are grand. It works on them. But not us. We're fucked.

Martin   No, I'm going to walk. They won't let me go home until I can walk.

Brendan   What's your name anyway?

Martin   Martin.

Brendan   You can forget about going home, Martin. This is your home now. High ceilings, long corridors, the smell of antiseptic and enough holy water to drown a bag of kittens. Pleased to meet you. I'm Brendan.

Martin   I'm going to walk!

Brendan (*indicates his wheelchair*)   They'll eventually get fed up and give you one of these. It's deadly. I was never so delighted the day they let me sit into it. I couldn't let on, of course. Oh no, they want you to feel like a failure, the fuckers. But it's not our fault. It's our muscles. Our muscles are shite. I heard the doctors saying it.

Martin   Our muscles?

Brendan   The older we get, the worse they get.

Martin   I don't believe you. They wouldn't bother with this if that was true.

Brendan   But sure they think they can fix anyone. And the more of us they fix, the more they can shake the box for Little Willie. Do you know what we are? I heard one of the sisters saying it. We're bad PR.

Martin   PR?

Brendan   Poxy Rejects.

He wheels himself about in his wheelchair. His arms are weak, so it's not exactly the showcase he intended.

But we're not the problem. They are. They go around in their white coats like they're perfect. And as for the nuns . . . You know what the sister did one day? She let out a fart.

Martin   She did not!

Brendan   I came back from breakfast when she was making my bed only she didn't notice I was there. And she lets off this terrible fart. And me right behind her and my face at arse-height.

Martin   Did you hear it?

Brendan   No, that was the thing. It was completely silent. Jesus, I nearly collapsed. Only I couldn't say anything, could I, cos you can't give out to a nun for farting. Which I think is wrong. Because they do.

Martin *is laughing.*

Brendan   Anyway, I'm going away as soon as I turn eighteen.

Martin   Where to?

Brendan   America. I heard the doctors talking about it, about how great it is over there if you're in a wheelchair. You've heard of the Vietnam War, yeah? Well, loads of American soldiers came back with their legs blown off and all the doctors tried to get them walking again, but the Vietnam vets said how the fuck can we walk if we've no legs to walk on? The doctors didn't know what to do with them. The Vietnam vets were sitting at home all day bored out of their heads. So they got together and grabbed their guns and told the politicians they'd shoot them if they didn't make it so they could go everywhere in their wheelchairs. And they did. They got rid of all the steps into the buildings and on buses, so there was nothing to stop them going wherever they wanted. They stopped trying to cure the crips and cured the buildings and the buses instead . . . Do you want to come with me?

Martin   Me?

Brendan   They love the Irish over there. We can pretend we're Vietnam vets and that some kind of chemical weapon fucked us up. Napalm maybe. Yeah, napalm.

Martin   I don't want to leave my family, Brendan. It's going to work. I'm going to walk. Wait! Where are you going?

Brendan *wheels himself away.* **Martin** *lies there.*

Martin   Brendan? Brendan? Get the sister! I need to go to the toilet . . . Brendan!

But no one hears him.

Scene Four

St Mary's a year later. **Vinny**, *a care worker, is pushing* **Martin** *to the toilet.*

Martin   Thanks, Vinny. I'm bursting.

But **Vinny** *suddenly stops.*

Martin   Ah, Vinny, please. I'm desperate.

Vinny   Yeah. A desperate culchie pain in the hole.

He lights a cigarette.

Martin   I drank too much tea.

Vinny   And whose fault is that?

Martin   If I wet myself –

Vinny   Don't even think about it.

Martin   – you'll have to clean me up and get me changed.

Vinny   You think you have a God-given right to have people running around after you?

Martin   Vinny, please. I can't hold it.

Vinny   Go on then. The jacks is just there.

Martin   I can't. You know I can't.

Vinny   You can't or you won't?

Martin *tries to move his wheelchair with his arms, but it's futile.*

Vinny   I don't know why they bother with the likes of you. You deserve to end up in one of those for the rest of your pathetic life.

Martin   I can think of worse things.

Vinny   You want to be in a wheelchair? Have you no shame? Thank God I'm not like you.

Martin   I'd rather end up in a wheelchair than end up a bollocks like you.

Vinny   Is that right? Well, at least I can go to the jacks.

Martin   Vinny, come on –

Vinny   You shouldn't even be allowed drink tea. Do you know how much time I waste each day bringing you lot to the jacks, pulling down jocks, wiping arses? And for what I'm paid?

Martin   Vinny –

He wets himself,

Vinny   For fuck's sake, you're after doing that on purpose.

Martin   No, I swear. My muscles – they're just not able. I'm sorry –

Vinny   Fuck this.

He starts to leave.

Martin   Wait, where are you going? You can't leave me here like this.

Vinny *throws his cigarette butt onto the floor and stamps it out.* **Martin** *sits there, sitting in a pool of his own piss, his arms too weak to move his wheelchair.*

Vinny   If you tell anyone – the sister or anyone – I will make your life a living hell. Got that?

Martin *nods. But* **Vinny** *leaves.* **Martin** *sits there, wet, helpless and humiliated. After a few moments,* **Brendan** *enters, pushing his chair slowly. He looks at* **Martin***, who looks away, ashamed.*

Martin   Can you get someone, please, Brendan?

Brendan   I'll get Vinny. I saw him just now –

Martin   No, not Vinny. Someone else.

Brendan   It was him, wasn't it? The prick. You have to tell her.

Martin   No –

Brendan   Martin –

Martin   If I say anything . . .

Brendan   What if he did this to someone else? What if it was me? You can't let people like that . . . you have to fight.

Martin   I can't fight. I can't do anything.

Brendan   Yes, you can. You've got a tongue, haven't you? Most important muscle in the body. You. Have. To. Fight. Look at me. Look at me! You can't let this go.

A silence as **Martin** *wrestles with this.*

Martin   Will you come with me?

Brendan *nods.*

Scene Five

St Mary's. **Martin, Sister** *and* **Vinny.**

Sister   Get out.

Vinny   Now wait a minute –

Sister   Get out, I said.

Vinny   You believe him? You believe him over me?

Sister   Get out or I shall call the guards.

Vinny   I'm going to get you, you little fucker. I'm going to break your fucking neck.

Martin   Go on then.

Vinny   You should have been flushed down the jacks the minute you were born. You're nothing but a burden. You're never going to do anything and when you die your family will celebrate.

Martin   You are a small man with a small heart and you couldn't be more wrong about me. I'm going to do things.

Vinny   Like what?

Martin   I'm going to America with Brendan.

Vinny   On your hole.

Martin   We're going to have adventures.

Vinny   Bollocks.

Martin   We're going to change the world.

Vinny   Change the world? You can't even change your own jocks.

Martin   Yeah, well, maybe I don't want to.

Sister   Get out, you pathetic little shit.

Vinny *goes.* **Sister** *turns to* **Martin***, who is shocked she used such language.*

Martin   Did you just say pathetic little –

Sister   That . . . That was the word of the Lord . . . I want to thank you for coming forward, Martin. You have saved countless other children . . . you have done this institution a great service.

Martin   Sister?

Sister   Yes?

Martin   Where's Brendan? He said he'd be here.

Sister   I wouldn't rely on Brendan, Martin. He talks a good talk.

An awkward silence between **Martin P** *and* **Brendan P**.

Brendan P   That's not fair. You know I would have been there, but –

Martin P   It doesn't matter.

Brendan P   – I was losing power in my arms. I couldn't get anyone to push me. (*Beat. Decides to come clean.*) I got Liam to bring me into the TV room. It cost me a bag of sweets. I hid there till I was sure Vinny was gone.

Martin P   I know. Liam told me. I bribed him with a comic. (*Beat.*) If it wasn't for you, I wouldn't have stood up to him. It was my fight, not yours.

Brendan P   It was mine too. I should have been there. I'm sorry, Martin.

Martin *is silent.*

Brendan P   I couldn't believe you actually went ahead and did it.

Martin P   Fuckin' eejit that I was!

Brendan P   Were you there a long time after I left?

Martin P   Years.

Scene Six

St Mary's. It's many years later, the 1970s. **Martin** *and* **Sister** *arguing.*

Martin   I'm telling you it doesn't work.

Sister   And I'm telling you it's our policy and we're not changing it. The best minds in this hospital decided –

Martin   I'm not saying they're not experts in medicine, but that doesn't mean they've got a clue about . . . They don't know what it's like to be handicapped.

Sister   This conversation is over.

She is about to push him off-stage.

Martin   So Liam was sent out to the local youth club last week, yeah? Only then he comes back in the next day saying he's never going back.

Sister   Why?

Martin   The woman that runs it, she said to them, 'Now this is Liam. He's from the hospital. Now you be good to Liam.'

Sister   Good.

Martin   No. Not good.

Sister   I don't understand.

Martin   She got him a cup of tea and a plate of biscuits, but when the other kids asked for tea and biscuits, she gave out to them. So only Liam got tea and biscuits.

Sister   Maybe the other kids had already had tea and biscuits?

Martin   Then she gave him first go at the table-tennis table and told him he could play as long as he wanted, even though they always take turns.

Sister   It sounds like she made him feel very welcome.

Martin   No, she made him feel like a tit.

Sister   Martin, please. *Special*. She made him feel special. But he is special. You all are.

Martin   But if you send us out to places and we're treated like we're special, the normal kids are going to hate us.

Sister   But handicapped children, as a compensation for their ailments, deserve to be treated –

Martin   Look, I've got an idea. Let me set up a sports club. Bring the normal kids in here. Let them use the facilities – the swimming pool, the hall, the gym. Let them mix with us like we're the same as them, only on our turf.

Sister   I don't know, Martin. That could be a bit much for some of our more vulnerable patients.

Martin   But aren't the doctors always talking about the therapeutic value of sport for handicapped children?

Sister   That's true, I suppose.

Martin   And if you let me run it, you'll have someone to blame if it's a disaster.

Sister   You know you're getting very disruptive, Martin. Why can't you just leave things as they are? Why are you always challenging everything?

Martin   Because what else am I supposed to do? Sit in the TV room all day sucking sweets?

Sister   Okay, I'll let you try this sports club. But if it doesn't work, you're to stop fighting us. It's hard enough running a hospital without resistance from your own patients.

Martin   And that's another thing. I'm not a patient. I'm not sick.

Sister   It's just a figure of speech.

Martin   No, it's not.

Brendan P   Jesus, look at you. When did you get so stroppy?

Martin P   What was I supposed to do?

Brendan P   I dunno. Chase girls? Are there any girls in this story?

Scene Seven

St Mary's. **Martin** *is looking at* **Josie,** *who is smoking.*

Brendan P   The smoker? Forget it. You've got no chance with her.

Josie *notices* **Martin.**

Josie   What do you want? Can't you see I'm busy?

Martin   No. Are you?

Josie   It's none of your business.

Martin   It is actually. I'm in charge of recreation.

Josie   Yeah, well that's what I'm doing. Recreating. Recreationing. Doing recreation.

Martin   I'm not sure smoking counts as recreation.

Josie   I'm not smoking. I'm not just smoking, I mean. I'm also, you know, observing.

Martin   Oh yeah? What are you observing?

Josie   You know, sport and stuff.

Martin   Will you give me a drag of that?

Josie   Do you smoke?

Martin   Come on, quick, before the sister sees.

She gives him a drag of her smoke. He coughs.

Josie   Look, what do you want? Seriously.

Martin   You're making me look bad.

Josie   What?

Martin   You're meant to be joining in.

Josie   I'm only here cos the teacher made me.

Martin   You don't want to be here? Why – do you hate cripples?

Josie   No –

Martin   Sister, sister, this girl hates cripples!

Josie   Stop, will you? I do not hate cripples.

Martin   Relax, I'm only pulling your leg.

Josie   Fuck's sake, Martin.

Martin   Oh you know my name, do you?

Josie   Sure everyone knows your name. You're 'the man' around here.

Martin   Am I? Yeah, I suppose I am.

Josie   Well, if you're going to be all cocky about it –

Martin   Shut up and give me another drag.

Josie   You're very full of yourself, aren't you?

Martin   You mean for someone in a wheelchair? Sister, sister –

Josie   Shut up, for fuck's sake.

Martin   So how about a game of table tennis?

Josie   What – against you?

Martin   Against one of the polio lads over there. A crip who can use his arms.

Josie   No thanks. Table tennis is stupid.

Martin   Football?

Josie   Stupid.

Martin   Swimming?

Josie   Swimming? You must be joking.

Martin   Why – cos it's stupid?

Josie   No, cos it's retarded.

Martin   Retarded? Are you calling me – sister, sister –

Josie   No, sorry. Jesus.

Martin   You can't swim, can you? Let me teach you.

Josie   You?

Martin   Do you want to learn?

Josie   I don't like the water.

Martin   Why – because it's wet?

Josie   No, because there's no air in it.

Martin   I can teach you. I can tell you what to do.

Josie   Yeah, I know. I've seen you do it.

Martin   Ah, so that's what you're observing?

Josie   I do want to learn, yeah. But I don't want everyone laughing at me.

Martin   They won't laugh at you. I promise.

Josie   What if I start drowning? Are you going to jump in and save me?

Martin   No.

Josie   No? And you expect me to –

Martin   But the lifeguard is.

Josie   Oh yeah, the lifeguard. Forgot about him.

Martin   Will we give it a go so?

Josie   I don't like people doing stuff for me for free.

Martin   It's my job. It's what they pay me peanuts to do.

Josie   Yeah, but can I do something for you?

Martin   You could buy me cigarettes.

Josie   No, something else.

Martin (*embarrassed*)   Something else?

Josie   You think I mean –

Martin   No –

Josie   You do! I can tell by you.

Martin   No, honestly –

Josie   You think I'm that kind of girl?

Martin   No, please –

Josie   Teacher, teacher –

Martin   No, no!

Josie (*laughing*)   Relax, I'm only pulling your leg.

Martin   Fuck's sake.

Josie (*joking*)   Like, who'd want to kiss a cripple anyway?

Martin   Yeah.

He is silent, hurt. He tries to laugh it off, but she can see she pushed the joke too far and has hurt his feelings.

Josie Jesus, fuck, I'm sorry. I thought we were having – I meant it like a joke.

Martin It's grand. You're grand.

Josie I didn't mean it, Martin. I swear. You're ten times better looking than most of the fellas here. I mean . . .

Martin It's okay.

They are both embarrassed.

What do you want to do in return for me teaching you to swim?

Josie Oh. This.

She gets behind his wheelchair and pushes him around in it. She stops and faces him.

Josie If you want, like.

He smiles, delighted by the sudden freedom.

Brendan P So you got what you always wanted – a woman to push you around!

Martin P It was amazing. It was freedom. All of a sudden I didn't have to wait any more. I could do things when I wanted.

Brendan P Who cares about that? Did you ever . . .?

Martin P Ever what?

Brendan P Get the ride, like?

Martin P Don't you get it? I was independent.

Brendan P Fuck independence. You fancied each other.

Scene Eight

St Mary's. **Josie** *is pushing* **Martin** *after her first swimming lesson.*

Martin   Think of your hand as a spear. Let it pierce the water.

Josie   Pierce the water? Okay.

Martin   It's a downward motion. And you need to keep your legs long, ankles loose, toes pointed.

Josie   Legs long, ankles loose, toes pointed.

Martin   Don't worry, it was only your first lesson. You'll get there.

They see **Mick** *sitting alone in his wheelchair, shivering.*

Josie   Hey, Martin, there's your man that was doing the float – the fella that had the clothes peg on his nose. What's wrong with him?

Martin   He looks cold.

Josie   No, I mean . . .

Martin   Oh, he's a Pug.

Josie   A Pug? Isn't that a breed of dog?

Martin   No, Poor Unfortunate Gobshite. It's from the guy that wrote *My Left Foot*, Christy Brown. He's one of the cerebral palsy lads. I always get nervous when I see him floating in the pool like that.

Josie   Why?

Martin   If he goes down, who's going to go after him? Who's going to give him the kiss of life? Not me anyway. Come on, let's go over.

Josie   Go over? Are you sure?

Martin   Why not? If he's going to be using my pool, I need to know who he is.

Josie   It's just, I heard him talking earlier.

Martin   So?

Josie *pushes* **Martin** *over to* **Mick**.

Martin   So, I'm Martin. What's your name?

Mick   Mick.

Martin *looks at* **Josie**. *Neither understand.*

Martin   Say again.

Mick   Mick.

They still don't understand him.

Josie (*pushing* **Martin** *away*)   Right, nice to meet you.

Martin   Josie.

Josie *stops.*

Martin   Mick?

Mick   Fuck's sake, about fucking time.

Martin   Do you want a scarf?

Mick   Why would I want a scarf?

Martin   Because you're cold. Waiting for a carer to bring you home? Josie, go out to the car park. You'll find his carer asleep on the special bus, on the doss as usual.

Mick *softens, impressed that* **Martin** *bothered to take the time to talk to him.* **Josie** *puts the scarf around* **Mick** *and exits.*

Martin   I always think you're going to drown when I see you in the pool. Would you not invest in a pair of armbands, no?

Mick   Sure I want to die, don't I? It would put me out of my misery.

Martin   I don't blame you, a Poor Unfortunate Gobshite like you.

Mick   That fucking Christy Brown. Hey, want to hear a joke?

Martin   A joke? Go on so.

Mick   What's this?

He moves his left foot rapidly up and down his crotch. **Martin** *is clueless.*

Mick   Christy Brown having a wank!

Martin   Christy Brown having a wank?

They laugh. **Albert** *wheels himself over in his wheelchair. He's a paraplegic, who wheels himself freely thanks to his powerful arms.*

Albert   That's it, Martin. Just smile and nod your head. That's what I do too.

Martin   What?

Mick *laughs at* **Martin***'s bemused reaction to* **Albert***.*

Albert   Sure God love him, and he's always in such good form. And do you know something?

Martin   Yeah?

Albert   He always remembers your name. And he's so appreciative of anything you do for him.

Mick   Will you do something for me now?

Albert *smiles and nods his head.*

Albert (*to* **Martin**)   See? Just smile and nod.

Mick   Fuck off.

Martin   I think he just told you to fuck off.

Albert   He's just so grateful and so happy and so . . . what's the word? Inspirational. Wouldn't we all love to be like that?

He leaves.

Martin   You're always in such good form. And you always remember his name.

Mick   And I always remember his. I call him 'bollocks'.

Martin   'Bollocks'? Yeah, that's what I'll call him too.

Mick *and* **Martin** *laugh.*

Scene Nine

St Mary's. Some years later. **Martin** *and* **Sister.**

Sister   You're leaving? But where are you going to go?

Brendan P   America? Thank God. Finally.

Sister   But, Martin, we have another group of children about to start. They need someone to look up to, someone to guide them –

Martin   Isn't that what you're here for?

Brendan P   Good answer.

Sister   Not someone like me. Someone like them.

Martin   If I stay, if they start depending on me, it'll be another ten years before I can get away.

Sister   But what's wrong with that? It's a job, isn't it? How many people with your condition can say they have employment?

Martin   I want to do something different.

Sister   Like what?

Martin   I want to travel. I want to see New York. I want to see the Grand Canyon. I want to look up at a Californian redwood. I want to sit in the back of a convertible and drive down Route 66.

Brendan P   And go to a ball game and eat hot dogs and drink beer and –

Sister   But all of that takes money.

Martin   Yeah, but I've got a job.

Sister   In America?

Brendan P   Of course in America. Where else? (*To* **Martin P**.) Have you?

Martin   No, here. Running a garage for some of the guys I met in this place. One's a mechanic, one's a panel-beater and the other one owns a workshop. But they need a manager. Once I've enough saved, I'm gone.

Sister   I really don't know about this.

Martin   I need to get away from disability. I've done my bit. I want a normal life.

Brendan P   Hot dogs, beer, pizza, girls –

Sister   But who's going to push your chair? Have you given any thought to that?

Martin   Josie.

Sister   Josie? But isn't it about time that Josie got a job of her own?

Martin   I can't think of a more important one. Can you?

The **Sister** *exits, disapproving.* **Josie** *comes on pushing* **Mick**.

Josie   Martin, you've got a visitor.

Martin   How are you, Mick? Any jokes?

Mick   I'm here on business this time.

Martin   Sounds serious.

Mick   I'm organising a meeting. Will you come along?

Martin   A meeting? What about?

Mick   Everything.

Martin   Everything? That could take a while. Will there be drink at it?

Mick   If I bring the Pugs, will you bring the Muscies?

Martin   Will I bring the Muscies? Ah, so you just want me for my van, is that it?

Mick   Deal with it. Some people just want me for my body.

Martin *laughs.* **Josie** *pushes* **Mick** *off-stage.*

Brendan P   Look, this is all very interesting, but can we cut to the bit where you actually go to America?

Scene Ten

Pandemonium as everyone is talking at once. **Martin** *and* **Josie** *are in attendance, along with* **Ursula** *(muscular dystrophy),* **Mick** *(cerebral palsy) and* **Dermot** *(cerebral palsy).* **Martin** *and* **Ursula** *sit side by side.* **Dermot** *stamps his foot to get everyone's attention.*

Mick   So I invited you all here today . . .

Brendan P   Wait a minute? What's this? Who are these poxy rejects?

Ursula *(leaning into* **Martin***)*   What's he saying?

Martin   Shhh. Will you give him a chance?

Ursula   We'll be here all night.

Mick   . . . to talk about the situation –

Ursula   Did you catch that?

Martin   I would if you'd let me listen.

Mick   . . . we find ourselves in.

He looks around to see if he's been understood.

Martin   Sorry, Mick, I –

Dermot *starts to translate – but he's also got a speech impediment.*

Dermot (*less severe speech impediment*)   He said I invited you all here today . . .

Ursula   And what did he say?

Martin   I think he said what Mick said.

Ursula   But what did Mick say?

Martin   I don't know what Mick said because you keep distracting me. Will you let the man say what he's trying to say?

Ursula   But I don't know what he's trying to say!

Martin   That's why you have to listen!

Mick   Will you please let me speak!

Brendan P   Martin, why are you showing me this?

Martin P   Cos that's how it started.

Brendan P   How what started?

Ursula   Martin, what did he say?

Dermot   He said, would you please let me speak!

But **Martin** *was too distracted by* **Ursula** *to catch what* **Dermot** *said.*

Martin   Mick, would you mind saying it again?

Ursula   No, don't make him say it again. We'll never get out of here if he says it again!

Dermot   For fuck's sake!

Martin   Look, can I do the translating? Is that okay with everyone?

Mick *nods.* **Dermot** *grudgingly concedes.* **Ursula** *shrugs.*

Mick   I invited you here today . . .

Martin   I invited you here today . . .

Mick   To talk about the situation . . .

Martin   To talk about the situation . . .

Mick   . . . that we find ourselves in.

Martin   That we find ourselves in.

Ursula *is doing her best to be patient, but her tolerance level is close to breaking point. Same with* **Brendan P**.

Brendan P   Seriously, can we not fast forward this bit?

Mick   I decided to bring . . .

Martin   I decided to bring . . .

Mick   . . . these two groups together . . .

Martin   . . . these two groups together.

Ursula   I'm sorry to interrupt, but Martin already explained why you wanted to bring us together. Because we're the two groups – people with muscular dystrophy and people with cerebral palsy – with the most in common –

Martin   Alright, Ursula –

Dermot (*giggling*)   The Muscies and the spas!

Martin   The Muscies and the spas? I thought it was Pugs?

Ursula   But if we know all that, why's he telling us again?

Mick   I'm just trying to set the scene

Martin   He's just trying to set the scene.

Ursula   I thought the purpose of this meeting was for each of us to talk about the things we want to change. That's why we're here, isn't it?

Mick   If you're not going to listen to me . . .

Martin   If you're not going to listen to me . . .

Mick   . . . then we might as well go home now . . .

Martin   . . . then we might as well go home now . . .

Ursula   Alright. Sorry, Mick.

Mick   You go first.

Martin   You go first.

Ursula   Me? Oh okay, thanks. Look, sorry for . . . I'm just so pissed off with things . . . So I've got a boyfriend. (*The lads start teasing and wolf-whistling.*) His name is Jimmy. He's non-disabled. We want to be together, like any normal couple. But I'm living in a home and . . . like, for example, I can't get up when I want to get up because I have to wait my turn. Because there aren't enough carers. And I can't go to the toilet when I need to go for the same reason – because I have to wait. In the summer, I'm put to bed at 4.30 because there aren't enough staff on to put me to bed later. It's crazy. 4.30 on a summer's day when most people are outside enjoying the sun. We want our own place, but it's very hard to find anywhere that's accessible.

Silence. **Ursula** *has finished.* **Dermot** *suddenly pipes up.*

Dermot   We need transport that's accessible.

Martin   Sorry, what's your name again?

Dermot   Dermot.

Martin   Dermot. Say again.

Dermot   Dermot!

Martin   No, sorry, what you were saying about transport.

Ursula   But what about what I just said? Aren't we going to talk about it?

Dermot   We need transport that's accessible.

Ursula   Hello. Housing?

Martin   We need transport that's accessible.

Ursula   We need housing that's accessible.

Martin Alright, Ursula. Noted.

Dermot When I get the bus –

Martin When I get the bus –

Dermot Stop fucking doing that!

Martin Not everyone can understand you, Dermot.

Dermot Then tell them to make a fucking effort!

Martin Then tell them to make a fucking effort?

Dermot I don't want some smug fucker I've never met translating my words!

Martin You don't want some smug fucker you've never met translating your words?

Dermot Fuck's sake! Stop, I said!

Silence. **Martin** *decides to hold his tongue. But as* **Dermot** *speaks, it's clear that most people are struggling to understand him.*

Dermot When I get the bus, I have to get out of my wheelchair. And crawl up the steps. My clothes get ruined. And sometimes the fucking driver won't even lift my chair on for me. It's a disgrace. It's a fucking disgrace.

He looks at the group, hoping they understood him. It's clear that they didn't.

Fuck's sake! (*To* **Martin**.) Go on then.

Martin When I get the bus, I have to climb out of my chair and crawl up the steps. It destroys my clothes. And the drivers don't always lift my chair on for me. (*To* **Dermot**.) Did I get all that?

Dermot The fucking drivers.

Martin The fucking drivers. Sorry, Dermot.

Dermot But I'm sick of special buses.

Martin I'm sick of special buses.

Dermot   And the way people stare at you like you're an animal in a cage.

Martin   And the way people stare at you like you're an animal in a cage.

Dermot   We need double-decker buses that are low-floor and accessible.

Martin   We need double-decker buses that are low-floor and accessible.

Dermot   Buses that everyone can use.

Martin   Buses that everyone can use.

Ursula   Houses that everyone can use.

It's clear from the silence that **Dermot** *has finished speaking.*

Ursula   What about you, Martin? What would you change? Oh sorry, I forgot. You're going to America.

Brendan P   Damn right he is. So you can all shove your revolution or whatever you want to call it up your –

Mick   So what do we do? If we want to change things, how do we go about it?

Martin   So what do we do? If we want to change things, how do we go about it?

No one seems to know.

Ursula   Should we set up our own organisation?

Brendan P   Come on, Martin, let's get out of here.

Martin   There's no point. There's already enough disability organisations out there.

Dermot   Yeah and they're all run by non-disabled fuckers or super crips!

Martin   And they're all run by non-disabled fuckers or super crips!

Ursula   What's a super crip?

Martin   You know those aquired injury fuckers like Albert who got their disabilities through car accidents and the like and then try to prove they're superhuman by doing marathons and climbing mountains and making the rest of us look bad?

Ursula   Oh, those guys. Yeah, they always seem to get the cushy jobs in disability. Is that what you call them – super crips? What does that make you – crips with chips on your shoulders?

Dermot   I do not have a fucking chip on my shoulder!

Ursula   Look, whatever, what do we need to do?

Silence. People don't know what to do.

Martin   If you ask me, you need to get on to the existing organisations and get your issues onto their agendas.

Ursula   'Your issues'?

Martin   Our issues.

Ursula   And how do we do that?

Martin   You write to them. You meet them. You lobby them. You shame them. You do whatever you have to do to make them notice you.

Mick   How do you know this stuff?

Martin   How do I know this stuff? Doesn't everybody?

Ursula   No.

Brendan P   Well, now you do. So good luck and *bon voyage*.

Scene Eleven

Martin's *council house*. **Martin** *and* **Josie**.

Martin   Go on, show it to me.

Josie   No way, it's desperate.

Martin   It couldn't be worse than mine.

Josie   You look good in yours.

Martin   Ah, but that's the point. You've seen mine, but I haven't seen yours.

Josie   So it's not fair, is it not?

Martin   Exactly. We're all about equality in this house.

Josie   Okay, but promise you won't laugh.

Martin   I won't. I promise.

Josie *shows him her passport photo.*

Josie   I knew it. You think I look funny.

Martin   You don't look funny. If anything you look serious.

Josie   You have to look serious. They reject it if you don't look serious.

She snatches it back and closes the passport.

Martin   There's nothing wrong with it.

Josie   I'm funny-looking. I know I am.

Martin   You're not funny-looking. You happen to have a nice smile.

Josie *is silent.*

Martin   Why do you give yourself such a hard time? Are you not going to answer me?

Josie   Are you looking forward to America?

Martin   Are you?

Josie   Can't wait. Just the chance to be someone else.

Martin   Someone else?

Josie   Ah you know, just somewhere new, where people don't know you.

Martin   When I went from Spiddal to Baldoyle, I thought I was going to be someone else. I thought I was going to walk.

Josie   So what are you saying to me – I'm going to be just like this in America?

Martin   Just like what?

She is silent.

Josie   How come someone like you, who can't do anything, can do so much, and someone like me, who can do so much, can't do anything? Why can't I do anything? What's wrong with me?

Martin   Nothing. Absolutely nothing.

Josie   You know, Martin, for a fella that can't raise his arms, you always manage to lift me. (*Beat.*) Jesus, I can't believe I said that.

Martin   Yeah, but you know why that is, don't you, why I can lift you? (*He grins madly and starts singing to the tune of 'He Ain't Heavy, He's My Brother' by The Hollies. He finishes with:*) She ain't heavy – she's my carer.

Josie (*laughing, embarrassed*)   Stop, will you?

They both laugh. They look at each other, smiling. A silence in which anything could happen.

Martin   Carer doesn't sound right, does it?

Josie   It's hardly like you need to be cared for.

Martin   Helped?

Josie   Assisted?

Martin   Personal assistant?

Josie   Personal assistant. I like that. Now that sounds like a job I could get used to.

Martin (*singing*)   She ain't heavy – she's my PA.

Josie   PA? Very good.

Martin   I'm remarkable. What can I say?

She laughs, really enjoying his company. The doorbell rings. Neither of them wants to break the moment.

Martin   Leave it. Let them come back tomorrow.

The doorbell rings again.

Martin   Fuck's sake.

Josie   Will I answer it?

Martin   Please.

Josie *goes off-stage and returns pushing* **Ursula**.

Josie (*off*)   Ursula, hi.

Ursula (*off*)   Is Martin in? Can you give me a push?

Josie *pushes* **Ursula** *over to* **Martin**.

Ursula   Martin, hi. Sorry for calling so late.

Josie   You're welcome.

A look between **Ursula** *and* **Josie**.

Martin   How did you even get here?

Ursula   Jimmy.

Martin   Where is he? Tell him to come in.

Ursula   I asked him to wait in the car. I need to talk to you in private.

She is self-conscious around **Josie**.

Josie   I knew there was something. You're out of milk. Will I pop out to the shop?

Martin   Thanks.

Ursula   Take your time.

Josie *gives* **Ursula** *a look and then leaves.*

Ursula   Does she tuck you in at night as well?

Martin   What do you want, Ursula?

She is surprised by his sharpness.

Ursula   Nice place.

Martin   The council took pity on me. 'Ah, God love him, the poor cripple.'

Ursula   I thought you hated charity?

Martin   I couldn't wait to get out of that hospital.

Ursula   Did I hear right that you've got a job?

Martin   I'm running a garage.

Ursula   What do you know about cars?

Martin   Nothing. But I know a bit about people.

Ursula   I thought you'd be in America by now.

Martin   Soon. Got my passport today.

Ursula   It must be great to be out of disability.

Martin   People still ask Josie if I want sugar in my tea.

Ursula   Must be great to have Josie.

Martin   I've got two other people as well.

Ursula   Three carers? All to yourself?

Martin   Personal assistants.

Ursula   What's the difference?

Martin   I need assistance, not care. I'm not a child. I'm not sick.

Ursula   But why do they do it? What's in it for them?

Martin   I pay them out of what I earn in the garage.

Ursula   So you're working for free?

Martin   It allows me to keep my benefits.

Ursula   Smart. Your own house, your own van and your own team of . . . care – personal assistants. Must be great to have everything figured out.

Martin   I'm thinking there must be a pretty good reason why you went to the trouble of coming all the way over here to the depths of the Northside.

Ursula   I've got some news. Jimmy and me, we've found a place. It's perfect. Fully accessible.

Martin   Congratulations. I'm delighted for you.

Ursula   I can't do it, Martin. I can't move in with him.

Martin   Why not?

Ursula   What if we have a row? What then?

Martin   But you two never have rows.

Ursula   We have rows all the time. We had one today. That's why I'm here.

Martin   Then kiss and make up.

Ursula   When we have rows, I need to be alone.

Martin   And what's wrong with that?

Ursula   I can't be alone in a flat. What if I need him? To get me dressed. To put me to bed. To bring me to the toilet.

Martin   Okay, so you're not allowed to row. Surely that's a small enough sacrifice for the sake of a place of your own?

Ursula   Couples need to be able to row.

Martin   What do you want me to say?

Ursula   It's not just if we row. What if Jimmy gets sick? How can I manage if I don't have any back-up? In the care home, I can ask a carer to help. Okay, I might have to wait an hour, but at least I won't be left there all night.

Martin   So you're institutionalised?

Ursula   For God's sake. Do I have to spell it out? The things we met to talk about – accessible housing, low-floor buses – they're no good to us without . . . They're no good to us without what you have: personal assistance.

Martin   Then that's what you need to fight for.

Ursula   I don't even know how to fight. None of us do. Except you.

Martin   Ursula, I'm going to America.

Ursula   Martin, there's a group of us that wants change. The Muscies and the Pugs. The lowest of the low. We're so far down the ladder that there is no ladder. They just want to leave us there to rot. How are you going to feel if you're off sunning yourself in California knowing you could have made a difference, but just left us behind?

Scene Twelve

Martin *and* **Albert**.

Albert   Can they not make do with a home help a couple of hours a day – you know, to get them up out of bed and sit them in front of the television and then put them back to bed at night? An hour in the morning and an hour in the evening.

Martin   And what are they meant to do for the rest of the day?

Albert   Ah, Martin, are they seriously asking for someone – their very own carer – for eight hours a day?

Martin   Not eight, no.

Albert   Thank God. What – four?

Martin   Twenty-four. And it's personal assistant, not carer.

Albert   Twenty-four? Are you off your rocker? Can you imagine the cost?

Martin   We're not asking you to pay for it. We're asking you to make an application to the EU under the Horizon programme on behalf of this particular group of disabled people.

Albert   Ah Martin, you have to be realistic.

Martin   Realistic? Do you even know what reality is? It's having to rely on your mother or father or sister or brother to get you up, get you washed, get you dressed –

Albert   Yes, I know, and it's very unfortunate.

Martin   It's having to wait an hour for a carer to bring you to the toilet.

Albert   Is that not what nappies are for?

Martin   Look, Albert, you've done well for yourself. You've risen up the ranks. But your organisation is supposed to act on behalf of wheelchair-users.

Albert   And that's exactly what we do.

Martin   What are we then – the ones that don't count?

Albert   No, of course not, but –

Martin   But we're supposed to be grateful for any bit of help we get?

Albert   But why shouldn't you be grateful for it?

Martin   So that's what you think of us? So your answer is no? You're not going to support us?

Albert   Look, it's different for you. You're not like the others. Be glad of your volunteers, Martin, and keep them sweet.

Martin   What about Mick?

Albert   But sure God love him, how could Mick cope with the responsibility of managing people? It would drive the poor fella half cracked.

Martin   Have you ever even had a conversation with Mick?

Albert   I talk to Mick all the time.

Martin   No, a conversation. As opposed to smiling idiotically, saying something patronising and then wheeling yourself away as fast as you can.

Albert   Sure how can I have a conversation with him when I can't understand him?

Martin   Have you ever bothered trying to understand him?

Albert   He can barely – he can't even tie his own laces, and I don't mean that in a bad way.

Martin   Can I tie my own shoelaces?

Albert   No, but you're –

Martin   Am I independent?

Albert   Well, not physically, no, but –

Martin   Do you even know what independence is? No, you don't, because you still believe all that rehab shit. Independence is choice. Independence is being in control of how things are done. Like I am. And like Mick, mark my words, is going to be.

Albert   Yeah, well, good luck with that.

He leaves. **Martin** *is furious.*

Martin   Josie, punch the wall.

Josie　Calm down, Martin.

Martin (*roars*)　Fuck!

Josie　Don't let him get to you. You're not going to change people like that. This is why you need to get away. This is why you want to escape to America.

Brendan P　She's right. You've got to listen to her. You've got to.

Scene Thirteen

A meeting of the Muscies and CPs. Among them **Martin**, **Ursula**, **Mick** *and* **Dermot**.

Brendan P　Oh not these handicaps again. That's it, I'm out of here.

But he stays to watch.

Ursula　Our own company? But I thought we said – agreed –

Martin　It's the only way.

Ursula　But what do we know about running a company?

Mick　I heard on the grapevine that Horizon have another deadline this year. Something about an underspend.

Martin　Perfect. Who do I need to talk to?

Ursula　Wait – what's perfect? What did he say?

Martin　The Horizon programme. European money. This is our shot.

Ursula　Our shot – at what?

Martin　At funding a personal assistance service.

Ursula　But who'd run it?

Martin　We will.

Brendan P   Oh Jesus.

Ursula   But we're not qualified. Shouldn't we talk about this?

Martin   We are talking about it.

Ursula   We need to make collective decisions –

Martin   I'm telling you what we need to do.

Ursula   And I'm telling you that we need to discuss the pros and cons and –

Martin   If you want me to lead, let me lead.

Ursula *is silent as she struggles with this.*

Dermot   What about public transport?

Martin   What good is public transport if people can't even get out of bed in the morning?

Ursula   You're right. We have to go for it. Oh my God, are we really going to do this?

Brendan P   Why couldn't you just go? You could have made a life for yourself over there. Why did you have to saddle yourself with all those other handicaps?

Martin P   What does it matter? What do you care?

Brendan P   Because surely one of us should have followed our dream?

Martin P   I didn't stop trying, you know. I still wanted to go.

Brendan P   And did you?

Scene Fourteen

Martin *and* **Ursula**. **Josie** *is watching closely, eager to leave with* **Martin**.

Ursula   It's wonderful news, Martin, of course it is.

Martin   This is what you've wanted, Ursula. Personal assistance. Now you've got it. For two whole years.

Ursula   But what will we do then?

Martin   Then?

Ursula   You're talking about something that's going to change my life, our lives, the lives of everyone that takes part.

Martin   But that's what's great about it.

Ursula   But after two years, are things going to go back to the way they were? Back to that tiny box room in that care home? Having to be put to bed at 4.30?

Martin   Those days are over.

Ursula   Yeah, for a while.

Martin   Okay, yeah, officially it's just for two years, but that's just what it says on the contract. That's just to get our foot in the door. In reality, once this starts, it's never going to stop.

Ursula   You mean they'll continue funding the programme after that?

Martin   Course they will.

Ursula   Did they say that? . . . They didn't, did they?

Martin   Okay, look, we couldn't ask for more than two years because they only fund for two years. Besides, I didn't want to scare them off. They've never seen anything like this before. It's a game changer. We have to ease them into it.

Ursula   And now that we have the money, we have to do what we said we'd do. We have to run this programme and run it well. We have to make a success of it.

Martin   That's why I need people like you.

Ursula   So I'm one of the guinea pigs, am I?

Josie   Now if you'll excuse us, please, Ursula, Martin has a bag to pack.

Ursula   Okay, I'll do it, I'll take part –

Martin   Brilliant.

Ursula   But on one condition. Stay. Don't go to America.

Martin   Ursula, I've already delayed –

Ursula   Show us what it means to be independent. Teach us how to train our PAs. Run the programme for us and do it so well that it will convince them that it has to keep going on a permanent basis.

Martin   Josie, come on, we're going.

Ursula   I mean it, Martin.

Martin   I'm going and that's the end of it.

Ursula   I'm scared, Martin. Excited, yes, but absolutely terrified. We all are. You're the only one of us who knows how to do this. Please.

Martin P *turns to* **Brendan P**. **Brendan P** *is reflective, lost in his own thoughts.*

Martin P   What? What's wrong?

Brendan P   I could have gone, couldn't I? To America. If I'd had someone like Josie.

Martin P   No.

Brendan P   No?

Martin P   Because you'd have been one of us, Brendan. You'd have been there from the start and you'd have stayed and fought with us.

Brendan P   One of the Muscies. I'd have liked that.

Martin P   Can you see why – why I had to see it through?

Scene Fifteen

Martin *is trying to recruit. He's talking to* **Sean**, *a wheelchair-user in an institution.*

Brendan P   That smell. Are we back in St Mary's?

Martin P   I went to a lot of places like St Mary's.

Sean   But what if . . . what if I get it wrong?

Martin   There is no 'getting it wrong'. You're allowed to make mistakes.

Sean   But how do I even go about getting one of these – what's it called again?

Martin   A personal assistant. PA. You put an ad in the paper.

Sean   But what do I know about putting ads in the paper?

Martin   I can help you. Once people reply to your ad, you decide who to interview.

Sean   Interview? No one said anything about interviewing. How do I do that? How do I decide who to take on? What if no one wants to mind me?

Martin   No, not mind you. Work for you.

Sean   Work? For me?

Martin   Yes, because you're going to be in charge. You're going to be the boss.

Sean   But what do I know about being in charge? I've never been in charge of anything in my life.

Martin   All you need to know is what you want.

Sean   What I want? But I don't know what I want.

Martin   When you wake up in the morning, what do you do?

Sean   I don't do anything. I lie there.

Martin   You lie there and wait, don't you?

Sean   Yeah. For one of the carers to get me up.

Martin   Does it ever happen that you badly need to go to the toilet?

Sean   Not so much. I stopped drinking tea years ago.

Brendan P   Me too.

Martin   Do you miss it?

Sean   I love tea.

Brendan P   'Course you do. Tea is lovely.

Martin   What if you didn't have to wait for a carer? What if your personal assistant could get you up whenever you wanted?

Sean   Whenever I wanted?

Martin   And what if they got you the breakfast you wanted and dressed you in the clothes you wanted?

Sean   The staff would never allow that here.

Martin   But what if you had your own place?

Sean   My own place? And they lived there too – my personal assistant?

Martin   No, they'd come to your house to work for you.

Sean   And would they be there when I woke up?

Martin   They'd be there throughout the night and yes, when you woke up.

Sean   Would they not be exhausted?

Martin   You might have three PAs to cover three shifts over twenty-four hours.

Sean   Three PAs? Is that three ads I'd have to put in the paper? Three people I'd have to be in charge of?

Brendan P   No, three people to set you free.

Martin   Think of it this way. One of them could make you a pot of tea at night. The second could get you up in the middle of the night to bring you to the toilet. The third could get you up in the morning and make you another pot of tea.

Sean   But would they not be mad at me? For having to take me to the toilet all the time?

Martin   No one will be mad at you. You're talking about people whose job it will be to do what you tell them.

Sean   But what if one of them doesn't show up? What if I wet myself and can't get up? What if they forget about me and leave me there? What if they don't like me? What if they think I'm just a bossy cripple?

Martin   Sean, this is a good thing. It could change your life. You could do anything you want.

Brendan P   Do you not have a dream, something you really want?

Sean   I hate lying in bed waiting for someone to get me up. I hate having to wait to be brought to the toilet. I hate that it feels like they're doing me such a big favour when it's their job. I hate the corridors that go on forever. I hate the smell of disinfectant. I hate the food. I hate that it's never up to me what we watch on television. I hate that I can't dress like a punk and get my hair done in a Mohawk. I hate that I can't go out at night and look at the stars and howl at the moon. I hate that no one thinks I can do anything. I hate that no one knows I'm somebody.

Martin   Then show us. Show us who you are.

Sean   I hate that I'm so scared.

Martin   This is your chance. I'm offering you a chance.

Sean   Give it to someone else.

He wheels himself away. **Martin** *watches him go.*

Brendan P   Wait! Come back!

But **Sean** *is gone.* **Brendan P** *turns on* **Martin P**.

Brendan P   Don't you see? Doesn't that prove it? Nothing changes.

Martin P   You told me to fight, fight, fight.

Brendan P   What did I know? I was a kid.

Martin P   So you were just all talk? Is that it?

Brendan P   They don't want us. They pretend we belong, but they don't mean it. We scare them, they don't know what to say or do with us – we're freaks.

Martin P   Yeah and so we're locked away for our own protection. The worst thing of all is we've become used to it. But we don't belong in the shadows. Is it not better to be seen?

Brendan P   Life is short. You've got to –

Martin P   What? Hide?

Brendan P   The path of least resistance, yes.

Martin P   The coward's way out.

Brendan P   Fuck you.

Martin P   No, fuck you.

Brendan P   Don't you see? There isn't time to fight. If all you do is fight, when do you get to live?

Scene Sixteen

The Centre for Independent Living (CIL) office. **Dermot** *is typing a letter one finger at a time. Slowly. His PA sits on a chair reading a book.* **Martin** *enters with* **Josie** *and looks around.* **Martin's** *in a foul mood.*

Martin   Dermot, what are you doing?

Dermot   I'm writing a letter. What does it look like?

Martin   You're what?

Dermot   I'm writing a letter, I said.

Martin   I can't understand what you're saying to me.

Josie   He said he's writing a letter, Martin.

Martin   I didn't ask you what he said. I asked him what he said.

Josie   Yeah, but I'm telling you –

Martin   Is it your job to tell me what he said? No. Exactly. You're my PA, not his. (*To* **Dermot**.) What are you doing?

Dermot *doesn't understand what's going on.*

Martin   I'm asking you what you're doing.

Dermot   You know what I'm doing.

Martin   Why do you have a PA? You obviously don't need one.

Dermot *is silent. He is beginning to get the point.*

Martin   How long are you working on that letter?

Dermot   A while.

Martin   What?

Dermot   A while, I said.

Martin   Sorry, don't know what you're saying.

Josie   Martin.

Martin   Will you keep out of this? (*To* **Dermot**.) If you're on this programme, it's because you need a PA. If you don't need a PA, you shouldn't be on this programme. Do you want to be on this programme or not?

Josie Martin, for God's sake.

Martin (*to* **Josie**)   Are you deaf? Is that your disability?

Dermot I don't need a fucking PA.

Martin You don't need a PA?

Dermot It's different for you. You can't do a fucking thing. I can.

Martin I can make myself understood, can't I?

Furious, **Dermot** *charges over to* **Martin***, ready to explode.*

Martin One of the reasons you've got a PA is that you've got a speech impediment and no one knows what you're saying. Is that right?

Dermot But some people do. You do! You understand me.

Martin Sorry, didn't catch that.

Josie Martin, you've made your point.

Martin Jesus Christ, Josie.

Josie Why should he use a PA around you when you know exactly what he's saying?

Martin Because he's not going to be around me forever. Because he's got to go out there and deal with people. Non-disabled people who won't know what the fuck he's saying. They'll just smile and nod their heads and send him on his merry way and nothing will change. His job is transport officer. His job is to lobby CIE to make their buses accessible. The point about having a PA is it allows you to deal with the real world, the non-disabled world. How can he do that if people can't understand him?

Josie Okay, but there are ways of doing things –

Martin Go and wait in the van.

Josie What?

Martin   We'll talk about this later.

Josie *leaves*. **Martin** *turns to* **Dermot**.

Martin   Why aren't you using your PA?

Dermot   He can't understand me.

Martin (*to PA*)   Is that true?

Max   Sorry, what? I didn't . . .

Martin   That you can't understand him – is that true?

Max   It's just I'm still getting used to . . . like I'm sure with a bit of practice . . .

Martin   So is that what you're doing? Practising?

Max   But I didn't think he wanted me to help him.

Martin (*to* **Dermot**)   It's up to you to make your PA understand you. It's up to you to take the time to train him, to get him used to your voice.

Dermot *nods*. **Martin** *waits*.

Dermot   Can you give me a hand with this letter, please, Max?

Max   Can I . . .?

Dermot   Can you give me a hand with this letter?

Max   Oh the letter, sure. Sorry.

Max *comes over and sits at the computer.*

Dermot   Can you type up what I say?

Max   Can I . . .?

Martin   Can you type up what he says? For fuck's sake, it's not that hard.

Dermot   Look, he's doing his best, okay?

Martin (*to* **Max**)   Just listen to him. He's just a person trying to make himself understood. Just listen to him.

He nods. **Dermot** *dictates.*

Dermot   Can you meet with me and my colleagues?

Max *didn't get that, but he's too afraid to admit it. He looks nervously at* **Martin** *and back to* **Dermot**.

Dermot   Can you meet with . . .

Max   Can you meet with?

He types.

Dermot   . . . me and my colleagues.

Max   Me and my colleges?

Martin   Colleagues.

Dermot   Just leave us alone, okay?

Martin   We need results, Dermot. We need buses that are accessible. It's your job to make that happen. Okay, I'm going. Josie?

He looks around for **Josie** *and then remembers that he sent her out to the van.*

Martin   Max, can you push me out to the van?

Max *gets up right away.*

Dermot   Stay where you are, Max.

Max *hesitates in his chair.*

Dermot   My PA is busy. Get your own.

Martin   Dermot, for fuck's sake.

Dermot   Leave me alone. I'm writing a letter.

Martin   Do you really want me in here all day?

Dermot (*to* **Max**)   Go on so.

Max *gets up and pushes* **Martin** *out to the van.* **Dermot** *giggles to himself.*

Scene Seventeen

Later that evening. **Martin** *sits in his spare wheelchair while* **Josie** *fixes a puncture in his main chair.*

Martin   Good thing I have a spare.

Josie   Any idea where you got the puncture?

Martin   Must have gone over some glass.

Josie   I didn't see any. I'm always careful.

Martin   I know you are. It's not your fault.

Josie (*sharply*)   I know it's not my fault. I'm not responsible for all the broken glass on the streets of Dublin.

She works away in silence for a while.

Martin   Long day.

She works in silence, refusing to engage with him.

Martin   You've got a knack for this.

Josie   My father taught me.

Martin   He taught you well.

Josie   When I was younger, I wanted to open my own bike shop.

Martin   I'll run it for you if you want. Now that I've got a bit of management experience.

Josie   No thanks.

Martin   Fair enough.

Josie   No, just, I wouldn't be any good at it.

Martin   You might surprise yourself.

Josie   I don't think so.

Martin   Josie.

She keeps working.

Martin   Look at me.

She looks at him.

Martin   You could have your own bike shop if you want.
You'd be great at it.

Josie   How can you . . . You act like nothing happened
today. You tell me I can do anything.

Martin   You can –

Josie   I love the way you have taken all these people –
people who were living in care homes, people who were
dependent on their families, people who had no freedom,
no lives, no prospects, no futures, no dreams – or maybe
they had dreams but had no chance of going after them – I
love the way you have taken all these people and given them
a chance of a normal life. The sort of life the rest of us take
for granted. I love the way their lives are changing for the
better. That people are getting their own flats, looking for
jobs, going to college, going to the pub, going to the cinema,
meeting friends. And that's all thanks to you.

Martin   It's not thanks to me. It's –

Josie   And it's not just people in wheelchairs. I used to
think I could never do anything. But I can swim, thanks to
you. I can work as a PA, thanks to you. And now I think I
can open my own bike shop, thanks to you. This is what you
do. You give people confidence in themselves. You see what
they can do, not what they can't. And that's why I've got
something in common with those twenty-nine people. But
you can't treat people like the way you did today.

Martin   Well, maybe I've lived a different life to yours.

Josie   That doesn't give you the right . . .

Martin   Oh you want to lecture me on rights, do you?

Josie   It doesn't give you the right to walk all over people.

Martin   And I can walk now, can I?

Josie You're more capable than anyone I have ever met in my life. It doesn't matter that you can barely move a muscle in your body. You've got a tongue, haven't you? That's all you need.

He is silent. Her words have hit home. She walks away. He would love to go after her, but can't.

Martin Josie.

Josie What?

He hesitates, struggling for courage.

Martin Any chance of a cup of tea?

She goes to make it. **Martin** *is annoyed with himself.*

Brendan P Why didn't you tell her?

Martin P Tell her what? . . .

Brendan P You know . . .

Martin P Because I had things to do, alright?

Brendan P Is that all you ever did – things?

Martin P *is silent.*

Brendan P And did it work? Did it get you what you wanted?

Scene Eighteen

A board meeting. **Martin**, **Ursula**, **Mick** *and* **Dermot** *in attendance.* **Martin** *addresses his board. The atmosphere is subdued.*

Martin Look, it was worth a shot. At least they know we exist. At least they know we mean business.

Ursula So how are we supposed to get around?

Martin We need to go with a stop-gap solution, something to get people moving in the meantime.

Dermot   No, it'll send out the wrong message.

Martin   Where's your PA, Dermot?

Ursula   He said it'll send out the wrong message.

Dermot   We don't want special buses. We want public buses.

Martin   They won't give us public buses.

Dermot   That's why we have to keep fighting.

Silence. Tension in the room.

Ursula   You told us to turn up outside the Dáil for your birthday. You didn't tell us there was going to be a double-decker bus waiting there for us. A bus we couldn't get on to.

Martin   That was the whole point. To highlight the fact that the government doesn't see disabled people as members of the public

Ursula   Yes, I get it, Martin, but it would have been nice to know in advance that we were there for a transport protest and not a birthday.

Martin   What difference does it make?

Ursula   The difference is, we're members of this board. We need to know what's going on.

Martin   Sometimes it's not possible to tell everyone what's going on.

Mick   Not everyone, no. But us, yes.

Ursula   Not everyone, no. But us, yes.

Martin   Stop interpreting, will you? I can understand him, you know.

Ursula   Yes, well not everyone can and what he's saying needs to be heard.

Martin   So, you don't think I know what needs to be done?

Ursula   Martin, you're the only one that knows. That's why we're so dependent on you. But you can't keep doing things without telling us.

Martin   Okay then. I'll tell you this. We're setting up our own bus service. We're calling it Vantastic and we're running it from the office in Bolton Street.

Dermot   No! No way!

Ursula   We can't set up our own bus service. How are we going to pay for it?

Martin   Let me worry about that.

Ursula   This should be decided by a vote.

Mick   I agree.

Ursula   Mick agrees.

Martin   I know he fucking agrees . . . Look, people need this now.

Ursula   We're supposed to be working towards a more equal society, but if you can't even treat your own colleagues as equals –

Martin   Does anyone in here doubt my judgement?

Silence.

Grand. I'll be in the van having a smoke. Let me know the outcome of your vote.

Dermot   You just betrayed everything we're supposed to be fighting for.

Martin   How many months were you trying to get a meeting with those people?

Dermot   I'm the one who was supposed to be in charge of transport. The first job in my life and you had to come along and undermine me because it wasn't happening fast enough for you. Have you got any idea how that feels?

Martin *doesn't know what to say.* **Dermot** *wheels himself away.*

Martin (*lying*)   I didn't catch a word of that. Did anyone else?

Ursula   Every word.

Scene Nineteen

Martin *sits brooding in his wheelchair while* **Josie** *potters.*

Martin   Another sup, please, Josie.

She lifts a glass of whiskey to his lips. He takes a drink.

Martin   Sit with me, will you?

She sits.

Martin   Have a drink with me.

Josie   I'm working, Martin.

Martin   I want someone to get drunk with.

Josie   Then call one of your friends.

Martin   What friends? Anyway, you're my PA.

Josie   Exactly. Your PA.

Martin   Your job is to do what I tell you to do.

Josie   Don't be a fucking arsehole, Martin. My job is not to get drunk. And well you know it.

She gets up to start pottering again.

Martin   Another sup, please.

She sits down. She lifts the glass to his lips.

Martin   Now just sit there, will you? Stop getting up.

Silence. She's not happy.

Martin   You don't let me away with anything, do you? It's one of the things I like about you. You're making me a better man.

Josie   I don't know about that.

Martin   You're right. I'm too set in my ways to change.

Josie   No one's ever too set in their ways.

Martin   Really? So how would you like me to change? Another sup, please.

She lifts the glass for him to drink.

Josie   I'm not trying to change you, Martin.

Martin   No, but if you did. If you could.

Josie   You are who you are.

Martin   I do what I have to do. I can't help it if I live in the real world. And in the real world you have to fight. Fight, fight, fight.

She is silent. He realises she's not buying it.

Martin   Ah look, I don't know what I'm talking about . . . If you won't get drunk with me, will you at least share a smoke?

She looks for a cigarette, but can only find one. As she searches for it, he looks at her. She notices. When she notices, he looks away.

She lights up, smokes, puts it between his lips. They share it like this for some moments. She notices his tangled hair.

Josie   Jesus, the state of it.

She stands behind him and starts brushing the back of his head while they share the cigarette.

Josie   Do you ever get tired of fighting?

Martin   It's what I signed up for. If you're a wheelchair-user, you've got a simple choice: either you suck sweets in a corner and watch television all day or you try to change the world around you. And that's a full-time job. There ain't gonna be no magic pill in my day. I realised that a long time ago.

Josie   But what about other things?

Martin   Maybe other things are for other people.

Josie   That doesn't seem very fair. That doesn't seem very equal.

Martin *is silent. He's tired beyond belief and exhausted from relentless fighting. He's enjoying the feeling of the brush and her hands through his hair.*

Josie   What about America?

Martin   America . . . I'd jack it all in tomorrow, all this stupid fighting, if . . .

Josie   Yeah, right . . . If what?

Martin   Would you come with me?

Josie   'Course I would. You already know that.

Martin   No, I mean . . . I mean not as my PA.

Surprised, she looks at him.

Martin   I'm talking about a normal life, the sort of life other people lead. A place of our own. Our own business maybe. A bike repair shop. I'd run it and you'd fix the bikes. I dunno – somewhere in Boston maybe, or Queens in New York. We'd go to the deli each morning and come back with fresh bagels and coffee and have our breakfast before we'd start our day. And the shop would be at the back of the house, so we wouldn't have to go far. And in the evenings, after a long day, we'd look at the setting sun and drink cold beer and talk about the road trip we're going to do, across America. We'd take out maps and work out our route and get on the phone and book all these really funky motels. I love that word – motel. I think I could be a better person somewhere like that, living that kind of life. I wouldn't always be pushing and fighting with people and making decisions that no one else had any part of because any decisions I'd make I'd only make with you. Because you wouldn't be my PA any more. You'd be my . . .

He notices she is looking at him and very emotional.

I can't lean over and kiss you. So it's up to you. It's up to you.

She doesn't know how to say what she wants to say.

Josie   Jesus, Martin.

Martin   Look, forget what I said. Forget America. I'm drunk.

Josie   Martin, I . . . I can't. I'm your personal assistant. I work for you.

Martin   I know. I know. I'm sorry.

He is staring into space, humiliated.

Josie   I don't think I can work for you anymore.

Before he can object, she kisses him. He is surprised – and overjoyed that she has feelings for him.

Josie   I've always fancied you, you know.

Martin   I need to call a board meeting.

Josie   Not the line I was expecting.

Martin   To tell them we're leaving.

She smiles. They kiss. The phone rings.

Martin   Let it ring out. You're my PA. That's an order.

They laugh. They kiss. **Brendan** *taps* **Martin** *on the shoulder.*

Brendan P   When you're finished . . . So, what happened next?

Scene Twenty

The board meeting breaks in on the kiss.

Ursula   We've been trying to get hold of you all day. Why aren't you answering your phone?

Martin   There's something we need to tell you –

Ursula   We've reached the limit of our overdraft. The bank won't lend us any more.

Martin   What?

Ursula   We were only meant to have twenty wheelchair-users on our programme.

Martin   Yeah, so?

Ursula   We've got twenty-nine. Thanks to you.

Martin   Look, it's grand. I'll get a loan.

Ursula   You've also been using EU funds to subsidise our transport service.

Martin   Yeah, so that people can get around.

Ursula   That money was ring-fenced for personal assistance, not transport.

Martin   I'll try other banks. I'll go back to Horizon. I'll convince them we need an extension.

Ursula   We've already tried the other banks. We've already asked Horizon for an extension. They can't. It was a two-year pilot programme.

Martin *is genuinely shaken.*

Dermot   What did you need to tell us?

Martin *looks at* **Josie** *and is about to answer.*

Josie   Nothing. It can wait. It's not important.

Martin *feels desperate for* **Josie***, but also grateful to her.*

Martin   Look, I'm sorry. I'm sorry, but it's not over.

Ursula   How can it not be over if there's no money left to pay our PAs? You had no right –

Martin   We are where we are. And we're going to go right back to the way we were if we don't do something about it.

Ursula   Yes, we are, but you're not, are you? You've got your house. You've got your van. And you've still got your fucking American dream with your girlfriend there, haven't you?

Josie   I'm not his girlfriend. I'm his PA.

A look passes between **Martin** *and* **Josie**.

Ursula   You were more than happy to play roulette with our lives, but what about your own?

Martin   Mine? Mine could end any day. So could yours. We don't know how long we have, so we have to live now. We have to live now. I don't care if I spend every penny in the bank. Our assets are people's lives and how they're changing.

Ursula   We were supposed to do this properly. We were supposed to show them we could be trusted with their money. We, the people in this room, the board of the Centre for Independent Living. 'Nothing about us, without us', remember? Well, what about us?

Martin   It's time to fight, Ursula. But not with me.

Ursula   You told us, you promised us –

Martin   Look at your lives now. What would you rather – that none of this had ever happened? We're going to win this and I'll tell you why. Because we've got something to lose.

Ursula   Yeah, Martin, we have, but what about you? What have you got to lose?

Martin   More than you know. So let's fight. Let's fucking fight.

Ursula   Is that all you've got to say for yourself? Fight, fight, fight? Is that really all you know? Our lives were changing. It was working. But now . . . now it's broken . . . It's like you can't function unless the shit's about to hit the fan. So you drive things so hard that everything comes crashing down and then you have no choice but to fight – and neither do we. Well, maybe you can't function without a fight, but I can. All I wanted was a normal life.

Martin   And what about me? You don't think I want a normal life?

Ursula   I'm not sure you're capable of one.

Josie   Of course he is. If you'd only let him.

Ursula   And what's that meant to mean?

Martin   Josie.

Josie   Why is it always up to him? Look what he's done for you. Why don't you do something for a change instead of forever moaning and demanding more?

Ursula   I think it's you that wants more, Josie, not me.

Josie   We both want more. We all want more. What of it?

Ursula   Why can't you live your own life? Why can't you find your own dream instead of piggy-backing on his?

Josie *walks off.*

Martin   Josie! Josie!

Silence. **Martin** *waits, anxious. Are they going to support him or not?*

Mick   Tell us what to do.

Ursula   You're going to listen to him?

Martin   Please. Trust me. It'll work, I guarantee it. I got us into this mess and I know how to get us out of it.

Dermot   This is your last fucking chance.

Martin   We need to meet with anyone we can – TDs, senators, the Health Board, the Department of Health, politicians, journalists – anyone and everyone you know who might have some influence. And we need to tell them our stories.

Ursula   And if that doesn't work?

Brendan P   And did it?

Martin P   No. So we hit the streets. Back outside the Dáil again. We grabbed politicians as they went in and out. We told our stories over and over again. We harnessed the opposition and then got word that the Minister would be forced to deal with us. That meant he had to do his homework. Day turned to night. We ordered pizzas and sang songs and we waited.

A bell sounds.

Finally it was time. We went into the Dáil. They wanted us to watch the debate on video in a room, but we insisted on going up to the gallery. But there was only one lift, and it was hardly ever used. We went up in groups of two or three and I was terrified it would break down. Once we were all up there, we took up very definite positions and looked hard right into the government's eyes. We wanted to make this as difficult for them as possible. I knew they couldn't possibly say no to us.

Brendan P   And?

Scene Twenty-One

We have returned to the start of the play.

The viewing gallery of Dáil Éireann. **Martin**, **Josie**, **Ursula**, **Dermot** *and* **Mick** *eyeball the Minister for Health.* **Martin** *is confident to the point of smug; the others are anxious.*

Minister   . . . I have great sympathy for this group of people, but would also point out that the government simply cannot be held to ransom like this. And so it is with regret that my department must decline their request for financial assistance.

A long silence. **Martin** *stares in disbelief.*

Martin   No. No. Noooooooooooooooo!

Scene Twenty-Two

Outside the Dáil. Everyone is stunned, speechless, devastated.

Josie   Martin, they're all looking to you. They don't know what to do.

Martin   I just need . . . just a minute. I just need to be on my own.

Ursula, Mick *and* **Dermot** *withdraw.*

Josie   On your own?

Martin   Tell them I've got a plan.

Josie   Have you?

Martin   Make them believe it. I'll think of something.

Josie   Why won't you just talk to them?

Martin   Because I'm the one that . . . This is my fault, no one else's.

Josie   You're all in this together –

Martin   Just go and tell them to sit tight. I always think of something. That's all they need to hear.

Josie   You don't know what to do, do you?

Martin   Just leave me the fuck alone!

She leaves and **Martin** *is left alone on stage. He agonises. For the first time in his life he has absolutely no idea what to do.*

Brendan P *comes on.*

Martin   Brendan, what am I going to do?

Brendan P   Do you remember when you got your first wheelchair?

Martin   For fuck's sake.

Brendan P   Do you not remember, no? You were fifteen years old.

Scene Twenty-Three

St Mary's, many years ago. **Sister** *helps* **Martin**, *aged fifteen, into a wheelchair. He enjoys the feel of it.*

Sister   It's not something to be proud of, Martin. All your life you're going to carry the stigma of being in a wheelchair. A cripple. A handicap. And plenty of people will remind you of that. So I'd take that smile off your face if I were you.

Martin   Can I take it for a spin?

He tries to wheel the chair, but his arms are too weak.

Can you give me a push?

Sister   Martin, this is the whole point. You need to be able to manage for yourself. You need to be independent.

Martin   Ah, give me a push, will you? I want to show Brendan my wheels.

Sister   Brendan?

Martin   Yeah.

Sister   Has nobody told you?

Martin   Told me what?

Sister   I'm afraid Brendan is no longer with us.

Martin   What do you mean? Has he gone home to his parents?

Sister   He died peacefully in his sleep last night.

Martin *just looks at her.*

Sister   It's all too common with his form of disability, I'm afraid.

Martin   His form . . .? Muscular dystrophy?

Sister   Duchenne muscular dystrophy, yes.

Martin   But isn't that what I have?

Sister   We don't know yet, Martin.

Martin   He was only eighteen. Am I going to die when I'm eighteen?

Sister   I have to go now. I have to speak to his parents about the funeral.

Martin   We were going to go to America together.

Sister   Yes, well, I think he knew that was never realistic. His older brother also had Duchenne. He died at the same age. Brendan . . . he would have expected it.

She leaves. **Martin** *is heartbroken.*

Scene Twenty-Four

Martin *and* **Brendan P**. **Martin** *feels overwhelmed with grief.*

Martin   It was you that fucked me up. It was you that made me fight.

Brendan P   You stupid crip, Martin. You don't fight because I told you to. You fight because you're angry. No one told you how to live your life. You chose how to live your life.

Martin   What about America?

Brendan P   I knew I'd never make it to America. That's why I gave my dream to you. All I wanted was to run away.

All I wanted was to live. I just didn't have enough time. But you refused to run away. You stayed to fight. America wasn't your dream. This is your dream.

Martin   Why did you have to leave me?

Brendan P   I didn't want to.

Martin   Why did you have to leave me alone?

Brendan P   You're not alone now.

Martin   Of course I am. I am and I always have been and I always will be.

Brendan *leaves.*

Ursula   We're here, Martin.

Martin *realises that* **Josie**, **Ursula**, **Mick** *and* **Dermot** *have returned.*

Martin   I'm sorry . . . I don't know what to do. I don't know what to do.

Ursula   Then we'll tell you.

Dermot   We're not leaving.

Mick   We're staying.

Ursula   We're staying right here outside the Dáil. We're not leaving here till we get what we want.

Dermot   We'll chain ourselves to the gates if it comes to it.

Mick   We'll go on hunger strike if that's what it takes.

Martin   You're right. We have to stay. We can't give up. You're right.

The wheelchair-users are given blankets to keep out the cold as they settle in for the night. **Josie** *approaches* **Martin**.

Josie   We're not going to America, are we?

Martin   I think I belong here. I think I need to see this through. What about you?

Josie (*very torn*)   I don't know. I . . .

Martin   I think you should go.

Josie   I think I should go, too. I think I need to give that bike shop a go.

Martin   I'm going to need to find a new PA, aren't I?

Josie   I was never really your PA.

She kisses him and leaves.

Ursula   Are you alright?

Martin *nods.*

Ursula   We're going to win, aren't we?

Martin   We are because we have to.

Ursula   If they're not going to drown us at birth, they have to let us live, don't they? And by 'live', I don't mean stick us in homes and forget about us. I mean real living. Making choices, making mistakes, fucking things up, falling in love, having our hearts broken, following our dreams, falling over our dreams. All that fabulous, messy, risky stuff that means we're alive. And we have to play our part too. Because it's easier to hide. It's easier to be invisible. It's easier to sit there in front of the television. Living, real living, is absolutely fucking terrifying and risky and painful, but it's also thrilling and glorious and wonderful. That's what we need to go after. That's what we need to demand. That's what we need to make happen.

Dermot   Yes.

Mick   Yes.

Martin   Yes.

They each look out into the audience, fully alive to the ongoing struggle, the campaign united.

9 781350 370166